IMAGES OF WA

AXIS ARMOURED FIGHTING VEHICLES OF THE SECOND WORLD WAR

RARE PHOTOGRAPHS FROM WARTIME ARCHIVES

Michael Green

Pen & Sword
MILITARY

First published in Great Britain in 2018 by
PEN & SWORD MILITARY
An imprint of
Pen & Sword Books Ltd
47 Church Street
Barnsley
South Yorkshire
S70 2AS

ISBN 978-1-47388-704-6

Typeset by Concept, Huddersfield, West Yorkshire HD4 5JL.
Printed and bound in India by Replika Press Pvt. Ltd.

Pen & Sword Books Limited incorporates the imprints of Atlas, Archaeology, Aviation, Discovery, Family History, Fiction, History, Maritime, Military, Military Classics, Politics, Select, Transport, True Crime, Air World, Frontline Publishing, Leo Cooper, Remember When, Seaforth Publishing, The Praetorian Press, Wharncliffe Local History, Wharncliffe Transport, Wharncliffe True Crime and White Owl.

For a complete list of Pen & Sword titles please contact
PEN & SWORD BOOKS LIMITED
47 Church Street, Barnsley, South Yorkshire S70 2AS, England
E-mail: enquiries@pen-and-sword.co.uk
Website: www.pen-and-sword.co.uk

Contents

Dedication

The author would like to dedicate this book to fellow tank buff Frank Schulz for his help and support over the years with so many of the author's works.

Foreword

With this volume, Michael Green surveys the armoured fighting vehicles of the Second World War Axis powers that were not tanks. The vehicles are predominantly German, for the simple reason that the other countries concerned lacked variously the funds, materials and industrial base to field such machines in quantity. Although we often think of the tank as the predominant weapon of Second World War battlefields, it is worth remembering that the German army in 1943–44 took delivery of more non-tank fighting vehicles than the former.

Most of the types of vehicles described in the pages that follow continue to be developed and produced by the major armies of the world up to the present day. While the increasing sophistication of the automotive and electronic technology has altered their size and appearance, their mission requirements have remained essentially the same as those of the vehicles described and analysed by the author.

The brief and clear descriptions of these vehicles and their purposes help us understand the intricacies of combined arms warfare on land. In doing so, Michael Green has performed an excellent feat in bringing sound military history to the reader.

Kenneth W. Estes
Lieutenant Colonel, US Marines

Acknowledgements

The bulk of the historical images in this work came from the files of the now-closed Patton Museum of Armor and Cavalry. For the sake of brevity all those photographs will be credited as the Patton Museum. Former volunteers of the museum who made an extra effort to assist the author with picture support include Chun-lun Hsu and Don Moriarty.

Other historical images came via David Fletcher of the Tank Museum located in Bovington, England. Contemporary pictures of preserved and restored Axis armoured fighting vehicles were supplied by friends whose names will be found in the photo credits. A special word of thanks goes to fellow tank buff Ian Wilcox for his picture support.

As with all published works, authors depend on friends for assistance in reviewing their work. Especially helpful as always was Peter Shyvers. Yuri Desyatnik and Remco Caspers were kind enough to provide information on German military radios and their associated antennas.

Notes to the Reader

1. To simplify the text and prevent the reader from becoming overwhelmed by the German military nomenclature for its vehicles, the author has employed the English translations of vehicle names and their designations in the text wherever possible.
2. The chapter breakdown is an attempt by the author to group the vehicles by their primary role or function. However, in practice many vehicles fulfilled multiple roles and thus transcend these groupings.
3. Not all improvised German military vehicles have been included due to lack of space and suitable photographs.
4. References to the German army include not only the Wehrmacht but the Waffen SS and Luftwaffe (Air Force) ground combat elements as well.
5. Although the quality of some images may be substandard, these have been included due to their historical rarity.

Chapter One

Reconnaissance Vehicles

Knowing the location of the enemy and his strength has almost always been a key predictor of success on the battlefield. This led the Axis armies (especially the German army) to field a number of armed and armoured reconnaissance vehicles, both pre-war and during the Second World War. The usefulness of some of these platforms resulted in their conversion to a number of other roles such as internal security.

The armed and armoured reconnaissance vehicles of choice for the Axis armies, at least initially, tended to be wheeled armoured cars. This came about for a number of reasons, mainly their reduced complexity and subsequent simplicity of manufacture which allowed for higher production rates. Germany could also draw on its engineering and manufacturing base (including the workforce) for commercial automobiles and trucks for their production.

Background

During the First World War (1914–18) the German army fielded a small number of improvised and dedicated (designed from the ground up) armoured cars. They were destroyed by 1920 under the provisions of the 1919 Treaty of Versailles. Under that treaty agreement the post-war German army was restricted to a maximum of 100,000 men and permitted no aircraft or armoured fighting vehicles of any type.

However, the senior leadership of the immediate post-First World War German army rejected both their civilian government overseers and the provisions of the Treaty of Versailles. Plans were therefore made in secret to re-equip the army with modern weapons and vehicles when the opportunity arose. The organization tasked with preventing the German army from re-arming departed the country in 1927.

In the Beginning

Between 1932 and 1934 the German army took into service 147 units of the Machine-Gun Carrier Kfz. 13. The abbreviation code letters 'Kfz.' stood for *Kraftfahrzeug* (motor vehicle), with the following numerals being its inventory number. The two-man vehicle was armed with a machine gun and based on an existing 4 × 2 passenger car due to its availability and affordability. It was also nicknamed the 'Adler'

Frame Antennas

The large horizontal or slightly curved frame antennas on pre-war and early-war German armoured cars and other vehicles were employed for medium- and long-range radio sets. At the time of their introduction they were found to be the only workable solution for operating radios from moving vehicles. The higher the frame antenna was set on a vehicle, the better the antenna efficiency. The disadvantages of the frame antennas were their relatively poor efficiency for their size and cost, and their conspicuous appearance on the battlefield which often marked them for early destruction. The frame antennas were eventually replaced by vertical-rod antennas.

after the original builder or the 'bathtub' by those who served on the vehicle, due to its rounded open-topped design.

A non-armed version of the Machine-Gun Carrier Kfz. 13 was labelled the Armoured Radio Car Kfz. 14. The Kfz. 14 was fitted with a horizontal folding frame antenna, which encircled the vehicle's upper armoured body (superstructure). A total of forty-seven units of the Kfz. 14 were built. Both the Kfz. 13 and Kfz. 14 would see service with the German army during the 1939 invasion of Poland and the 1940 invasion of France before being withdrawn from front-line service in 1941.

Next in Line

The replacement for the Kfz. 13 was the Light Armoured Car Sd.Kfz. 221. The abbreviation Sd.Kfz. in a vehicle's designation stood for *Sonderkraftfahrzeug* (special-purpose motor vehicle). It was applied to most but not all German-designed and built military vehicle designations with the numerals following being the vehicle's inventory number.

Production of the Sd.Kfz. 221 ran from 1935 to May 1940 with 339 units completed. It was based on a modified 4 x 4 civilian car chassis to keep costs down and speed up its introduction into service. Armament consisted of a single machine gun mounted in a seven-sided open-topped turret. To prevent hand grenades from falling inside the vehicle, the turret was covered by a metal-framed two-piece wire mesh screen.

Some units of the Sd.Kfz. 221 were later up-armed to remain viable on the battlefield with a 28mm tapered-bore gun (also known as a squeeze-bore gun). It fired a tungsten carbide-core round. The weapon's breech had a calibre of 42mm and at the muzzle end it narrowed to 28mm. The use of the gun was discontinued by 1943 due to a shortage of tungsten carbide.

A modified model of the Sd.Kfz. 221 was referred to as the Light Armoured Car (Radio Version) Sd.Kfz. 223. It had a frame antenna and carried a stored crank-up sectional telescopic mast antenna that could only be employed when the vehicle was stationary. The Sd.Kfz. 223 had the same machine-gun-armed open-topped turret as that fitted to the Sd.Kfz. 221. A total of 550 units were constructed between 1935 and 1944.

Upgrading the 4×4 Armoured Car

The Light Armoured Car Sd.Kfz. 221 was superseded on the production line in 1936 by an up-gunned version designated the Light Armoured Car Sd.Kfz. 222. The vehicle was armed with a 20mm automatic gun and a coaxial machine gun in a new larger ten-sided open-topped turret. As with the preceding light armoured car, the turret was protected by an anti-grenade wire mesh screen. Production of the Sd.Kfz. 222 ended in June 1943 with a total of 989 units built.

In production from November 1940 until April 1943 were the unarmed Light Armoured Radio Cars Sd.Kfz. 260 and Sd.Kfz. 261. They were both variants of the Sd.Kfz. 222. The only differences between the two versions were the type of radios fitted and their respective antennas. One had a stored telescopic mast antenna and the other a frame antenna. A combined total of 493 units of the Sd.Kfz. 260 and 261 came off the assembly line.

Larger Armoured Cars

To complement the small 4 × 2 Light Armoured Car Kfz. 13 armed only with a machine gun and introduced into service in 1932, the German army brought into its inventory in the same year the first units of the Heavy Armoured Car Sd.Kfz. 231 (6-Wheel).

Based on a modified 6 × 4 commercial truck chassis, the Sd.Kfz. 231 (6-Wheel) was armed with a turret-mounted 20mm automatic gun and a coaxial machine gun. It had a driver's position in both front and rear hull (superstructure) to allow it to quickly withdraw when in a confined space that did not allow for turning the vehicle around.

A variant of the Heavy Armoured Car Sd.Kfz. 231 (6-Wheel) was the Heavy Armoured Car (Radio Version) Sd.Kfz. 232 (6-Wheel) fitted with a frame antenna. The combined total of the two vehicles built was 123 units by 1937. There were also twenty-eight units of a variant of the series labelled the Armoured Radio Car Sd.Kfz. 263 (6-Wheel). It had a non-rotating turret armed with a forward-firing machine gun. The vehicle also came with a frame antenna and a stored telescopic mast antenna.

The poor off-road performance of the 6 × 4 Heavy Armoured Car series led the German army to withdraw them from front-line service following the invasion of France in the summer of 1940 as a series of more capable replacements became available.

German Armoured Car Employment

From the US War Department Handbook on German Military Forces published in March 1945 appears this passage describing the tactical employment of German army armoured cars:

When a motorized reconnaissance column expects contact with the enemy, it advances by bounds. The length of bounds depends on the cover the terrain offers as well as on the road net. As the distance from the enemy decreases, the bounds are shortened. The Germans utilize roads as long as possible and usually use different routes for the advance and the return.

The reconnaissance battalion commander normally sends out patrols which advance by bounds. Their distance in front of the battalion depends on the situation, the terrain, and the range of the signal equipment, but as a rule they are not more than an hour's traveling distance (approximately 25 miles) ahead of the battalion. The battalion serves as the reserve for the patrols and as an advance message center (*Meldekopf*), collecting the messages and relaying them to the rear. Armored reconnaissance cars, armored half-tracks, or motorcycles compose the motorized reconnaissance patrols, whose exact composition depends on their mission and on the situation. Motorcycles are used to fill in gaps and intervals, thereby thickening the reconnaissance net.

When the proximity of the enemy does not permit profitable employment of the motorized reconnaissance battalion, it is withdrawn and the motorized elements of the divisional reconnaissance battalion take over. Divisional reconnaissance battalions seldom operate more than one day's march (18 miles) in front of the division, covering an area approximately 6 miles wide.

Armored car patrols normally are composed of three armored reconnaissance cars, one of which is equipped with radio. An artillery observer often accompanies the patrol so that in an emergency fire can be brought down quickly. This type of patrol usually is organized for missions lasting one to two days. Tasks are defined clearly, and nothing is allowed to interfere with the patrol's main objective. If enemy forces are met, action is avoided unless the force is so weak that it can be destroyed without diverting the patrol from its main task. If enemy action is anticipated, the patrol is reinforced with self-propelled guns and occasionally with tanks. Engineers and motorcyclists are often attached to the patrol to deal with road blocks and demolitions.

While scouting a woods a favorite German ruse is to drive the leading car toward its edge, halt briefly to observe, and then drive off rapidly, hoping to draw fire that will disclose the enemy positions. At road blocks, the leading car opens fire. If fire is not returned, men dismount and go forward to attach tow ropes to the road block. If necessary, the patrol dismounts and proceeds with machine guns to reconnoiter on foot. A patrol is never split up, but in open country distances between cars may be as much as 200 to 300 yards.

Dedicated 8×8 Armoured Cars

The German army had provided funding in 1929 to three German firms to experiment with the development of what was referred to as the Heavy Cross-Country Armoured Car. Two firms submitted 8 × 8 vehicles with the third a 10 × 10 vehicle. The two 8 × 8s showed promise but the German army decided in 1930 that the continued development of a dedicated armoured car design was too costly at that time.

With more funding becoming available in 1934, the German army once again sought a dedicated 8 × 8 heavy armoured car design. Using experience gained in the earlier experimental programme, German industry developed the Heavy Armoured Car Sd.Kfz. 231 (8-Wheel) and the slightly modified variant the Heavy Armoured Car (Radio Version) Sd.Kfz. 232 (8-Wheel) fitted with a frame antenna. A rod antenna began replacing the frame antenna on the vehicle in July 1942.

Both versions of these new 8 × 8 heavy armoured cars were powered by liquid-cooled gasoline engines. They were armed with a 20mm automatic gun and a coaxial machine gun in enclosed turrets. As with the previous 6 × 4 armoured cars, they had a driver's position in both the front and rear of their armoured bodies.

The combined total of the two versions of the 8 × 8 armoured cars built between 1936 and September 1943 was 607 units. Of the two types, the Sd.Kfz. 231 was only in production until 1942 when it was replaced by an upgraded diesel-engine-powered variant.

A related variant of the 8 × 8 armoured car series was the gasoline-engine-powered Armoured Radio Car Sd.Kfz. 263 (8-Wheel). It had a large enclosed upper superstructure topped by a frame antenna. It was also provided with a stored telescopic mast antenna. A total of 240 units were assembled between April 1938 and April 1943.

Up-Gunned

Combat experience early in the Second World War demonstrated to the German army that its armoured car inventory armed with 20mm automatic guns was under-gunned. This would result in the fielding of a number of up-armed variants of its 8 × 8 armoured cars to supplement the firepower of their more lightly-armed counterparts.

The first example of an up-gunned 8 × 8 armoured car placed into service was labelled the Heavy Armoured Car (75mm Tank Gun) Sd.Kfz. 233. As indicated in its designation, it was armed with a 75mm main gun that was labelled the 7.5cm StuK 37 (L/24).

The 7.5cm StuK 37 (L/24) was a short-barrel, low-velocity gun optimized for firing high-explosive (HE) rounds but also able to fire a hollow-charge round. Another

German 8×8 Armoured Cars in Action

From a Military Intelligence Service Information Bulletin published in December 1941 by the American War Department appears this translated story of a German army reconnaissance unit in action during the Battle of France in the summer of 1940:

After advancing for a distance of 125 miles, our division reached Langres on the evening of June 15 [1940]. There Lieutenant Prohl's patrol, consisting of two 8-wheel reconnaissance cars, was ordered to reconnoiter to the east for a distance of 35 miles and to blow up the railway line at the Jussey junction so as to block all transportation to the south. Since the pressure on the Maginot Line had become very strong, the French were trying to move part of their forces to the south. For this reason, the mission was extremely important and had to be carried out with the greatest care.

At 7:30pm the patrol left Langres. About eight miles to the east, our advance road crossed over the railway line coming from Jussey, and there we encountered the first transport train. When we first saw the transport train from an elevation just west of the crossing, we halted and took cover, letting it pass by undisturbed. After reporting this by wireless [radio] to the battalion, which the train was bound to meet on the way, we continued our advance. The highway between Hortes and Vitrey runs parallel to the railway for part of the way at a distance of 500 yards from it, and we met two other transport trains while moving along this road. The poilus [French soldiers] leaned on their elbows in the windows and looked at us with the greatest astonishment. We sent another message back to the battalion and sped past the trains at full speed, knowing that the battalion would be ready for them. It seemed almost as if the French had not been aware that we were Germans. Under no circumstances were we to take up the fight with them now or we would very likely fail to carry out our mission.

We drove on, having very little contact with the enemy, and arrived at the important junction of the highways Langres–Combeaufontaine and Bourbonne-les-Bains–Champlitte. On this highway, there was considerable vehicle traffic moving towards the south. We halted just before we reached the junction and remained under cover, waiting until the way was free. After a few minutes, we decided to cross over in spite of the fact that single vehicles were still passing. We reached the crossing just as two French trucks transporting about fifty soldiers came toward us from the north. As there were houses on either side of the street, neither of us had seen the other. We stood facing each other a few yards apart, and when the driver of the first truck saw the two reconnaissance cars facing him and the muzzles of the cannons pointed directly at him, he realized the futility of resistance, and the two trucks with their occupants became ours.

We quickly disarmed the fifty men and disabled the trucks by disconnecting the fuel feed. Since we could not take them with us, we left the French behind and continued on. In every village that we passed we found from 30 to 40 French soldiers. Many of them were sitting with inhabitants in the streets. They had unbuckled their belts, had laid their weapons aside, and had made themselves comfortable. They were so surprised on seeing us that they were not able to fire a shot. We disarmed almost 250 men, and at about 10.00pm arrived in Jussey, where we were to blow up the railway tracks. We had covered the 30 miles in 2½ hours.

Parking the reconnaissance cars in the shelter of the woods, we went over to the other side of the tracks, where the station was situated. The demolition point lay about 200 yards from the station and 50 yards from the edge of the woods. The No. 1 gunner of the wireless reconnaissance car remained at the edge of the woods with the sub-machine gun. The forward and rear drivers of the point reconnaissance car proceeded to the station master's house, a small building near the station, to protect the flank and cut the telephone lines. The two reconnaissance car commanders then proceeded to lay the explosive charges. While they were thus occupied, a transport train came rolling along another track several yards from them. It slowed down and to my horror I saw that the signal had been set at 'Stop'. I thought we were all lost, for the train stopped just in front of us. The French sprawled at the windows; one of them was playing a harmonica – the others were singing a song and looking at the countryside. I looked around to see if our four men were visible, but there was nothing to be seen of them. They had crouched down beside the tracks and, thanks to the approaching twilight, could not be distinguished in their black uniforms. Suddenly the tension was broken: the signal was raised and the train whistled sharply and rolled on. We all heaved a deep sigh of relief.

The explosives were quickly put into place and tamped, the fuze was set, and one minute later the charges exploded. Pieces of stone and iron were hurled through the air with a roar. The tracks had been torn apart. We had succeeded in disrupting the railway – the order had been carried out. We started on our way home, but in the meantime, it had become dark. Suddenly, to our right, we saw a white cloud of smoke rising up into the sky and, realizing immediately what it was, we halted and saw the transport train rolling slowly through the moonlit countryside. We caught it on our sights, and each of the reconnaissance cars fired a clip of shells into the boiler. An enormous column of smoke rose into the air and the train stopped. In this way, we brought three transport trains to a stop in a stretch of 2 miles. At 1.00am we arrived at the battalion without any casualties or damage.

Next morning, we drove again to Jussey. A few miles before Jussey we took several Alsatians prisoner. They told us that on the previous evening, after the railway tracks had been blown up, their lieutenant had sent out the whole company to search for the parachutists who had supposedly carried out this action.

name for such rounds is 'shaped charge' or in post-war American military lexicon Chemical Energy (CE), better known as high-explosive anti-tank (HEAT) rounds.

The 75mm gun on the 8 × 8 Sd.Kfz. 233 was the same weapon mounted on the early-production models of the *Panzerkampfwagen* IV (or Panzer IV for short) medium tank. It was mounted on the right-hand side of the vehicle's open-topped front superstructure with the driver on the left side of the front superstructure.

The initial ten production units of the Heavy Armoured Car (75mm Tank Gun) Sd.Kfz. 233 were converted in October 1942 from existing units of the Heavy

> ### Gun Designation Meaning
> The number at the end of a gun designation behind the forward slash (/) is the length of the weapon in calibres. The length of a gun in feet, for example, can be determined by multiplying the size of the bore (in this case, 3 inches or 75mm) by the calibre. Hence 3 × 24 is 72 inches, which converts to 6 feet for the gun length.

Armoured Car Sd.Kfz. 231 (8-Wheel) series. These were followed in turn by a total of 109 new-built units of the vehicle constructed between December 1942 and October 1943. These units were based on the Sd.Kfz. 231 series chassis powered by a liquid-cooled gasoline engine.

The Puma

Beginning in September 1943 the first production units of a redesigned version of the original Heavy Armoured Car Sd.Kfz. 231 (8-Wheel) came off the factory floor. It was armed with a long-barrel high-velocity 50mm main gun optimized for firing armour-piercing (AP) rounds. There was also a coaxial machine gun in the fully-enclosed turret. The vehicle was designated the Heavy Armoured Car (50mm) Sd.Kfz. 234/2. It was also officially nicknamed the 'Puma'.

The biggest design change with the Puma was the introduction of an air-cooled diesel engine in place of the liquid-cooled gasoline-powered engines that had powered all the preceding 8 × 8 heavy armoured cars. Other changes included a thickening of the armour and having the armoured body of the vehicle serve as its chassis (unibody). On the earlier gasoline-engine-powered 8 × 8 heavy armoured car models the armoured body was bolted to the vehicle's chassis (structural frame).

Initially the German army had envisioned ordering 1,500 units of the Heavy Armoured Car (50mm) Sd.Kfz. 234/2. However, in January 1944 that number was dropped to only 101 with production being terminated in September 1944. The up-armoured diesel-engine-powered chassis of the Puma would go on to become the standard for all future-built 8 × 8 heavy armoured cars in the German army.

Puma-based Chassis Variants

The direct replacement for the gasoline-engine-powered Heavy Armoured Car Sd.Kfz. 231 (8-Wheel) was the Heavy Armoured Car (20mm) Sd.Kfz. 234/1, powered by a diesel engine. It retained the same armament of its predecessor, but the gun was now mounted within a six-sided open-topped turret covered by a wire mesh anti-grenade screen. A total of 200 units of the four-man vehicle came off the factory floor between June 1944 and January 1945.

The diesel-engine-powered replacement for the gasoline-engine-powered Heavy Armoured Car (75mm Tank Gun) Sd.Kfz. 233 first came off the production line in June 1944. It was labelled the Heavy Armoured Car (75mm Tank Gun) Sd.Kfz. 234/3.

It retained the same short-barrel, low-velocity 75mm gun as its predecessor, but this was now centred in the front superstructure behind a gun shield. By the time production ended, a total of eighty-eight units had been completed.

In November 1944, at Hitler's insistence, the Heavy Armoured Car (75mm Tank Gun) Sd.Kfz. 234/3 had its short-barrel, low-velocity 75mm gun replaced. Instead a long-barrel, high-velocity 75mm towed anti-tank gun designated the 7.5cm PaK 40 (L/46) was modified to fit within the existing confines of the open-topped super-structure. That weapon was optimized to fire AP rounds.

Reflecting the armament change to the Heavy Armoured Car (75mm Tank Gun) Sd.Kfz. 234/3, it was relabelled the Heavy Armoured Car (75mm Anti-tank Gun 40) Sd.Kfz. 234/4. A total of eighty-nine of these diesel-engine-powered vehicles were completed between December 1944 and March 1945.

Half-Tracks

In 1939 the German army identified a requirement for three different types of armoured half-tracks. They would all be based on the shortened chassis of an unarmoured half-track prime mover. That vehicle was designated the Light Towing Motor Vehicle/1-Ton/Sd.Kfz. 10. It was also referred to as the 'D7'.

Of the three armoured half-tracks ordered, the first to enter service in early 1940 was labelled the Light Armoured Observation Vehicle/Sd.Kfz. 253. It was intended for use by assault gun units. A total of 285 units were built by June 1941. It was followed by the Light Armoured Ammunition Carrier/Sd.Kfz. 252, which came off the production line in January 1941 with 413 units constructed by September 1941. It too was intended for use by assault gun units.

The Light Armoured Personnel Carrier Sd.Kfz. 250/1 did not enter into production until June 1941. By the time its production concluded in October 1943, a total of 4,250 units had been built. To speed up production a simplified model designated the Sd.Kfz. 250/1 (New) began coming off the assembly lines in October 1943 with 2,238 units completed by 1944.

With the introduction of the Light Armoured Personnel Carrier Sd.Kfz. 250/1 (New), the original model was relabelled the Light Armoured Personnel Carrier Sd.Kfz. 250/1 (Old). Both the old and new versions of the Sd.Kfz. 250 series were modified to serve in a number of different roles.

Reconnaissance Half-Tracks

The Light Armoured Infantry Vehicle Sd.Kfz. 250 was intended to serve alongside armoured cars in reconnaissance units. It was fitted with a shield-protected machine gun at the front of its open-topped superstructure. There was also a pedestal for the mounting of a second non-shield-protected machine gun at the rear of the vehicle's superstructure.

Some units of the Sd.Kfz. 250/1 were armed with a non-shield-protected machine gun fitted to a tripod mount for more accurate and sustained fire at longer-range targets, including indirect fire. These same vehicles also carried a second machine gun that could be fired from a pedestal at the rear of the vehicle superstructure or dismounted and fired from a tripod mount stored on the rear of the half-track.

Due to the superior off-road capabilities of the Light Armoured Personnel Carrier Sd.Kfz. 250/1 compared to existing 4 × 4 light armoured cars, a variant designated the Light Armoured Infantry Vehicle (20mm) Sd.Kfz. 250/9 armed with a 20mm gun and a coaxial machine gun in an open-topped turret replaced the Light Armoured Car Sd.Kfz. 222 in 1943.

Up-Gunned Reconnaissance Half-Tracks

To supplement the firepower of the Sd.Kfz. 250/1 and Sd.Kfz. 250/9, several additional weapon-armed versions of both the Sd.Kfz. 250 old and new models appeared. These included the Sd.Kfz. 250/7 armed with an 81mm mortar and the Sd.Kfz. 250/10 armed with a forward-firing, high-velocity 37mm anti-tank gun.

A third weapon-armed model was the Sd.Kfz. 250/8. It was armed with a forward-firing, short-barrel, low-velocity 75mm gun. This was the same gun as mounted in the Heavy Armoured Car (75mm Tank Gun) Sd.Kfz. 234/3. The Sd.Kfz. 250/8 did not enter into production until late 1943.

Pictorial evidence also shows there were improvised weapon-armed versions of the Light Armoured Infantry Vehicle Sd.Kfz. 250/1. These would include the fitting of a captured French 25mm towed anti-tank gun and a German 50mm towed anti-tank gun minus their two-wheel towed carriages.

Because the 37mm gun on the Sd.Kfz. 250/10 was already obsolete by the time it was fielded and there were delays in fielding the Sd.Kfz. 250/8 with the 75mm gun, the German army decided as an interim measure to field the Light Armoured Infantry Vehicle (Anti-tank Gun 41) Sd.Kfz. 250/11. It was armed with a 28mm tapered-bore gun. If required, the tapered-bore gun on the vehicle could be dismounted and fired from a ground mount carried on the vehicle.

From a May 1943 American Military Intelligence Service Bulletin appears this passage regarding the Sd.Kfz. 250/11 armed with the 28mm tapered-bore gun:

It may be that this gun is a local improvisation. Firing forward, it is mounted on a light half-track, with a coffin-shaped armored body. The small weapon may be identified by its prominent muzzle brake and flat, double shield. The chassis is that of a 1-ton half-tracked vehicle. The battle weight is about 6 tons … The crew is believed to number five.

There were four sub-variants of the Sd.Kfz. 250/3 Light Radio Car, each with a different configuration of its radio depending on the type of unit with which it was to serve. The Sd.Kfz. 250/3 was employed by German army motorized units as command and control vehicles, and by the German Air Force as a platform for forward air controllers accompanying ground units. The frame antennas of the various sub-variants of the Sd.Kfz. 250/3 Light Radio Car were eventually replaced by rod antennas so they would not attract enemy fire as command and control vehicles.

Non-Reconnaissance Half-Tracks

By 1941, the German army decided that the Light Armoured Observation Vehicle/ Sd.Kfz. 253 and the Sd.Kfz. 252 ammunition re-supply vehicles employed by assault gun units were too costly to build and decided to replace them with more affordable modified versions of the basic Sd.Kfz. 250.

The Sd.Kfz. 253 was replaced by the Sd.Kfz. 250/4 and the Sd.Kfz. 250/5. The Sd.Kfz. 252 was replaced by the Sd.Kfz. 250/6 which existed in two sub-variants, differing only in the dimensions of the 75mm ammunition for which each was designed.

For self-propelled artillery units there was the radio-equipped survey and range-plotting model Sd.Kfz. 250/12. There was also a telephone cable-laying version for communication units designated the Sd.Kfz. 250/2. It had large reels holding telephone cables on each of its front mudguards and another in the rear superstructure. With this arrangement, the crew could lay out the telephone cable on either side of the vehicle as it advanced, or directly behind it.

Foreign Armoured Cars in German Service

Following Germany's annexation of Austria in March 1938, the Waffen SS took into service twenty-seven units of a heavy armoured car that had been delivered by automotive firm Austro-Daimler to the Austrian army and police between 1935 and 1937. The vehicle was armed with a 20mm automatic gun and two machine guns. It was labelled the Armoured Combat Vehicle (ADGZ) by the German military. In 1941, the Waffen SS ordered twenty-five additional units of the vehicle from Austro-Daimler for internal security duties. These were delivered in 1942.

With the fall of France in the summer of 1940, the German army acquired 360 units of the 4 x 4 Panhard 178 along with their spare parts. An additional 176 units were constructed for the German army during the follow-on occupation by French industry. The vehicle featured a 25mm automatic gun and a coaxial machine gun. In German army service it was referred to as the Armoured Car Panhard 178-P204(f), the (f) in the vehicle designation meaning that it was French-built.

Some 190 units of the Armoured Car Panhard 178-P204(f) were used by the German army during its invasion of the Soviet Union in the summer of 1941, with 107 units lost by the end of 1941. A small number were configured as radio cars with forty-three units modified to run on railroad tracks. In 1943, an unknown quantity were fitted with a newly-designed open-topped turret armed with a 50mm gun.

The German army sometimes employed small numbers of foreign armoured cars captured in battle to make up for its own chronic equipment shortages. As spare parts did not normally come with these captured vehicles, their usefulness was very limited. With that in mind many would be employed by the German army in the less demanding internal security role and discarded when they could no longer be kept running.

Hungarian Armoured Cars

Employed by the Royal Hungarian Army during the Second World War were eighty-one units of a 4 × 4 reconnaissance armoured car designated the 39M Csaba. The vehicle was armed with a 20mm automatic cannon and a coaxial machine gun. Also built were twelve radio-equipped command and control vehicles equipped with a frame antenna and referred to as the 40M.

The Hungarian army fought alongside the German army in the invasions of Yugoslavia and the Soviet Union in 1941. However, it was effectively out of the war by early 1944 when Hungary was occupied by the German army.

Italian Armoured Cars

With the outbreak of the Second World War the Italian army took the armoured bodies off a small number of First World War-era armoured cars and mounted them on the chassis of modern 4 × 4 trucks. The resulting vehicle was referred to as the 'FIAT-Terni Tripoli'. Armament consisted of a single Breda-SAFAT 12.7mm machine gun mounted in an open-topped turret. Of the eight to ten units constructed, all were lost during the fighting in North Africa between the British and Italian armies.

In 1937, the Italian army issued a requirement for a 4 × 4 reconnaissance armoured car. The end result was the machine-gun-armed AB40. The first production units appeared in 1941. Twenty-five were built before the Italian army requested an up-gunned variant armed with a 20mm anti-tank gun and two machine guns. That up-gunned model was labelled the AB41 with 550 units completed between 1941 and 1943. It would see extensive service with the Italian army from the Eastern Front to North Africa alongside the German army.

Upon the Italian government's surrender to the Western Allies in September 1943, the Germans rapidly occupied northern Italy to deny as much of the peninsula as possible to the Allies. They also confiscated all the Italian army's equipment within the German sphere of control. Included among the haul were approximately fifty units of the AB41 armoured car. In German army service it was designated the Light Armoured Car AB41 201(i) and employed in the internal security role. The (i) in the vehicle's designation meant that it was Italian-built.

Within the German army jurisdiction in northern Italy was the factory that had built the AB41 for the Italian army, as well as a redesigned and upgraded model of the vehicle designated the AB43. When Italy surrendered to the Allies, less than a dozen units of the AB43 had been built and never issued to the Italian army.

Upon its takeover of the factory for the AB43, the German army restarted production of the armoured car. A total of 120 units of the AB43 were built by the time production ended in 1945. It was employed by the German army as the AB43 203(i) – and by other Axis forces – in the internal security role until the conclusion of the Second World War.

Copying a British Armoured Car

Another reconnaissance car intended for use by the Italian army was named the 'Lynx'. It was an approximate copy of the British army 4 × 4 Daimler Dingo armoured car. However, only one prototype had been built when the Italian government surrendered and the factory that was to build the vehicle came under German army control. Impressed by the vehicle's capabilities, the Germans ordered the production line restarted and designated it the Armoured Reconnaissance Vehicle Lynx 202(i).

In the end, only 129 units of the Lynx were constructed between 1944 and 1945. Like the AB43, in German military service the Lynx was often employed in internal security duties. As with the original British vehicle, the Italian copy was open-topped and armed with a single machine gun. Some were employed by the military arm of the Italian Social Republic. This was a puppet fascist government supported by the German army in northern Italy between 1943 and 1945.

Japanese Armoured Cars

In the early 1920s, the British firm of Crossley had developed a 4 × 4 truck chassis upon which the British firm of Vickers mounted a machine-gun-armed armoured body. A number of these were purchased for British army use in India. This resulted in the vehicle being named the Crossley Indian Pattern Armoured Car. Two were subsequently sold to the South African army and a small number were bought by the Japanese navy for their naval infantry units. Pictorial evidence shows them in use in China during the 1930s.

A British-designed and built armoured car from the firm of Austin was tested by the Japanese army in the early 1920s but failed to impress. This led the Japanese automotive industry established in the late 1920s to design and build armoured cars. One of these was the machine-gun-armed 4 × 2 Type 92, which entered service in 1932. Introduced into service the following year was the machine-gun-armed Type 93 Sumida. It was a 6 × 4 armoured car that could be configured to ride on rails or on wheels. Both were employed in China primarily as internal security vehicles by the Japanese military.

In the 1920s, the only armoured vehicles allowed in Germany were weaponless armoured personnel carriers, an example of which is seen here. They were reserved for use by the German police on internal security duties. Referred to as Police Special Purpose Wagons, they had a crew of three and room for twelve passengers. This particular vehicle is fitted with a frame antenna. (*Patton Museum*)

In 1932, the German army felt sufficiently confident to defy the restricting provisions of the 1919 Treaty of Versailles and field its first armoured car design, seen here. Based on a 4 × 2 civilian car chassis, the vehicle was designated the Machine-Gun Carrier Kfz. 13. The two-man vehicle weighed approximately 4,200lb, had a top speed of 43mph and was protected by armour with a maximum thickness of 8mm. (*Patton Museum*)

(**Above**) Somewhere on the Eastern Front a German soldier stands watch on a Light Armoured Car Sd.Kfz. 221. It was the replacement for the Machine-Gun Carrier Kfz. 13. An identifying feature of the vehicle was the single direct-vision armoured flap on the front of the superstructure. Maximum armour thickness on the vehicle was only 8mm. Top speed was 56mph. (*Patton Museum*)

(**Opposite**) In this overhead picture of a Light Armoured Car Sd.Kfz. 221 we can see the very simple two-piece anti-grenade wire mesh screen. Combat experience made it clear that the vehicle's machine-gun armament did not offer sufficient firepower on the battlefield. Some units of the Sd.Kfz. 221 were therefore up-gunned with a 28mm squeeze-bore gun affixed to the original open-topped turret. (*Patton Museum*)

(**Above**) The Light Armoured Car (Radio Version) Sd.Kfz. 223 shown here was a variant of the Sd.Kfz. 221 Light Armoured Car. To make room for the vehicle's radio, the machine-gun turret was located further to the rear on the vehicle's roof. Note the frame antenna is in its folded-down position. The vehicle weighed approximately 9,900lb and had a length of 15ft 7in. Its width was 6ft 4in and height 5ft 7in. (*Patton Museum*)

(**Opposite, above**) Taking part in a parade are at least four of the Sd.Kfz. 223 Light Armoured Cars (Radio). Their frame antennas have been lowered and folded rearward. Beginning in May 1942 all new-built units coming off the factory floor had 30mm frontal armour. To compensate for the weight gain, they had more powerful gasoline engines fitted. (*Patton Museum*)

(**Opposite, below**) Pictured here is an unrestored Light Armoured Radio Car Sd.Kfz. 261. The wheels and their rims are not original to this vehicle. It is also missing its frame antenna, although the support posts for it can still be seen. Note that it has the single direct-vision armoured flap in the front superstructure, as did the Light Armoured Car Sd.Kfz. 221. (*Dean and Nancy Kleffman*)

The replacement for the Sd.Kfz. 221 Light Armoured Car was the up-gunned Sd.Kfz. 222 Light Armoured Car seen here. It came with a new larger open-topped turret armed with a 20mm automatic gun and a coaxial machine gun, which is not fitted on the vehicle shown here. The Sd.Kfz. 222 had authorized stowage for 180 rounds of 20mm ammunition. (*Patton Museum*)

(**Opposite, above**) A restored and operational Sd.Kfz. 222 Light Armoured Car. Until April 1942 the entire armoured body of the vehicle was only 8mm thick. Beginning in May 1942 the front of the armoured body was made 30mm thick on all new-built vehicles. To compensate for the extra weight imposed by the thicker armour the Sd.Kfz. 222 was fitted with a more powerful engine. (*Chris Hughes*)

(**Opposite, below**) The Sd.Kfz. 222 Light Armoured Car pictured here would be found in the reconnaissance battalion of tank (Panzer) divisions in their 1939 Table of Organization and Equipment (TO&E). Each reconnaissance battalion had two squadrons that were divided into three troops; two of the troops were equipped with six light armoured cars each. Each light armoured car troop was further divided into two three-car sections. (*Patton Museum*)

(**Above**) The consequences of having only 8mm thick armour on this Sd.Kfz. 222 Light Armoured Car are clear to see on the example shown here. What is interesting in this picture is the improvised spaced armour arrangement projecting out from the front of the vehicle's lower hull. This was not a factory-applied modification but no doubt built by the unit with which it served. (*Patton Museum*)

(**Opposite**) In 1929, German industry began the development of a 6 x 4 Heavy Armoured Car for the German army. To save time and money it was to be based on the modified chassis of an existing gasoline-engine-powered commercial truck rather than a dedicated platform designed and built from the ground up. Pictured here is one of the prototypes of the 6 x 4 Heavy Armoured Car. A design feature that appeared on the prototypes was a driver's position in the rear hull. Note the spare tyre attached to the inside of the vehicle's rear superstructure access hatch on this prototype. On the production units, the spare wheel sometimes appeared on the exterior of the rear superstructure access hatch. (*Patton Museum*)

Pictured here is a production Heavy Armoured Car Sd.Kfz. 231 (6-Wheel) taking part in a pre-war training exercise. It can be identified as an early-built unit as the 20mm automatic gun is on the left-hand side of the gun shield and the coaxial machine gun on its right. On later-production units the weapon arrangement was reversed and the direct-vision armoured flap was omitted. (*Patton Museum*)

The Heavy Armoured Car Sd.Kfz. 231 (6-Wheel) had a top speed of 44mph. There was authorized stowage for 200 ready rounds of 20mm ammunition on the vehicle and 1,500 rounds for the machine gun. It was not fitted with a radio. The vehicle height was 7ft 4in with a width of 6ft and a length of 18ft 3in. (*Patton Museum*)

In this photograph we see a Heavy Armoured Car (Radio Version) Sd.Kfz. 232 (6-Wheel). The frame antenna added an extra 2ft to the height of the vehicle. Due to the added weight of the frame antenna the vehicle's top speed was only 38mph. Range – as with the Heavy Armoured Car Sd.Kfz. 231 (6-Wheel) – remained at 155 miles. (*Patton Museum*)

The two-man turret crew of this Heavy Armoured Car (Radio Version) Sd.Kfz. 232 (6-Wheel) are posing for the photographer. Armour thickness on this vehicle – as it was for the Heavy Armoured Car Sd.Kfz. 231 (6-Wheel) – was a maximum of 8mm. The front-mounted engine made it very vulnerable to mobility kills by enemy fire or mines.

(*Patton Museum*)

(**Opposite, above**) The 6 × 4 heavy armoured cars were not the German army's first choice; rather they were what could be afforded at that time. What the German army had really wanted as early as 1927 was a dedicated state-of-the-art multi-wheel heavy armoured car. Pictured here is one of the two 8 × 8 experimental prototypes built for the German army's consideration that were eventually rejected due to lack of funding. (*Patton Museum*)

(**Above**) In this factory photograph of a Heavy Armoured Car Sd.Kfz. 231 (8-Wheel) appear the openings in the turret gun shield for its armament. From 1936 until April 1942 the thickest armour on the vehicle was on the front of the armoured body and turret at 15mm. The front armoured body on all new-built Sd.Kfz. 231 units was thickened to 30mm from May 1942 onwards. (*Patton Museum*)

(**Opposite, below**) On display at a German museum is this preserved Heavy Armoured Car Sd.Kfz. 231 (8-Wheel). The vehicle was armed with a 20mm automatic gun and a coaxial machine gun. Note the factory-built 8mm spaced armour arrangement attached to the front hull. With the thickening of the armour body on new-built vehicles starting in May 1942, the spaced armour arrangement was done away with. (*Frank Schulz*)

(**Opposite, above**) Somewhere in North Africa the British army has recovered an abandoned Heavy Armoured Car Sd.Kfz. 231 (8-Wheel), possibly for technical evaluation. The vehicle weighed 9.3 tons, had a length of 19ft 2in, a width of 7ft 2in and a height of 7ft 7in. Its top speed was 53mph on level roads and maximum range was 186 miles. (*Tank Museum*)

(**Opposite, below**) A derelict Heavy Armoured Car Sd.Kfz. 231 (8-Wheel) lies in the ruins of a bombed-out town. All eight wheels could be steered, giving the vehicle a much smaller turning radius for a vehicle of its size and therefore more manoeuvrability. That and the independent suspension system provided a dramatic improvement in off-road performance compared to the earlier 4 × 4 light armoured cars and the 6 × 4 heavy armoured cars. (*Patton Museum*)

(**Above**) Pictured here is the radio-equipped counterpart to the Heavy Armoured Car Sd.Kfz. 231 (8-Wheel) with its frame antenna. It was designated the Heavy Armoured Car (Radio Version) Sd.Kfz. 232 (8-Wheel). It retained the armament array of the Sd.Kfz. 231. Visible on the front fenders of the vehicle are auxiliary fuel tanks that were discontinued on later-production units. (*Patton Museum*)

(**Above**) A small number of the 8 × 8 heavy armoured car series were designed as command and control vehicles and fitted with frame antennas as seen here. In this configuration the vehicles were labelled the Armoured Radio Car Sd.Kfz. 263 (8-Wheel). In place of the 360-degree weapon-armed rotating turret of the other variants, the Sd.Kfz. 263 had a large fixed superstructure. (*Patton Museum*)

(**Opposite**) Seen here in North Africa with the German army is an Armoured Radio Car Sd.Kfz. 263 (8-Wheel) with its stored telescoping mast antenna erected. Note the crew has built small sand berms (barriers) in front of the vehicle's wheels to offer some protection from small-arms fire or artillery fragments. With the frame antenna fitted the Sd.Kfz. 263 had a height of 9ft 5in. (*Patton Museum*)

(**Above**) In response to what was being encountered on the battlefield, the German army entered into a constant process of increasing the firepower on its armoured cars. An example of this is the Heavy Armoured Car (75mm) Sd.Kfz. 233 pictured here. The 75mm gun is in a forward-firing position with 12 degrees of traverse either left or right and elevation of only 12 degrees. The 75mm gun could be depressed 10 degrees. (*Patton Museum*)

(**Opposite, above**) A Heavy Armoured Car (75mm) Sd.Kfz. 233 is shown here on patrol. The driver's direct-vision armoured flap is seen in the open position to the right of the 75mm gun mount. Located under the gun barrel is the driver's access hatch. There are smoke canisters affixed to the front fenders of the vehicles pictured. (*Patton Museum*)

(**Opposite, below**) American soldiers pose for the photographer on a captured Heavy Armoured Car (75mm) Sd.Kfz. 233. The three-man vehicle had authorized stowage for thirty-two rounds of 75mm ammunition. It was also typically armed with a non-coaxial machine gun. Note the crew access hatch in the lower hull between the two separate wheel fenders. There would be a duplicate on the opposite side of the vehicle. (*Patton Museum*)

(**Opposite, above**) Pictured here is a Heavy Armoured Car (50mm) Sd.Kfz. 234/1 captured by the British army in Normandy, France in the summer of 1944. Nicknamed the 'Puma', a prominent external design feature of the diesel-powered second-generation 8 × 8 heavy armoured cars is their one-piece wheel fenders. The front of the vehicle's superstructure and turret were 30mm thick. The Puma weighed approximately 26,300lb. *(Patton Museum)*

(**Above**) The 50mm gun mounted in the Puma was derived from the towed anti-tank gun seen here, designated the 5cm PaK 38 (L/60). Serviced by a five-man crew, the 1,800lb gun was only 3ft 5in in height. Firing its standard armour-piercing projectile at 2,739 feet per second (f/s) it could penetrate 59mm of armour sloped at 30 degrees at 574 yards. On the Puma, the 50mm anti-tank gun was labelled the 5cm KwK 39/1 (L/60). *(Pierre-Olivier Buan)*

(**Opposite, below**) In this picture we see a captured Heavy Armoured Car 20mm Sd. Kfz. 234/1 minus its armament of a 20mm automatic gun and coaxial machine gun. This diesel-engine-powered second-generation 8 × 8 armoured car weighed approximately 15,700lb. It was 19ft 7in in length, had a width of 7ft 9in and a height of 6ft 9in. *(Patton Museum)*

The battlefield usefulness of the gasoline-engine-powered Heavy Armoured Car (75mm) Sd. Kfz. 232 led to a modified version being based upon the new diesel-powered second-generation 8 × 8 armoured car as seen here. It became the Heavy Armoured Car (75mm Tank Gun) Sd.Kfz. 234/3 and was armed with the same 75mm gun as its predecessor. *(Patton Museum)*

Besides the one-piece wheel fenders on the armoured body of the Heavy Armoured Car (75mm Tank Gun) Sd.Kfz. 234/3, the diesel-powered second-generation model had its 75mm gun fitted into a new gun shield as seen on this preserved example. Another spotting feature of all the variants of the diesel-powered second-generation 8 × 8 armoured cars was the single-piece front bumper. *(Tank Museum)*

On Hitler's orders the firm building the Heavy Armoured Car (75mm Tank Gun) Sd.Kfz. 234/3 substituted a long-barrel 75mm gun for the original short-barrel 75mm gun. This re-arming resulted in the designation being changed to Heavy Armoured Car (75mm Anti-tank Gun 40) Sd.Kfz. 234/4. Pictured here is a preserved example belonging to the US army museum system. *(Dean and Nancy Kleffman)*

Rather than taking the time to design and build a new specific gun shield and gun mount for the Heavy Armoured Car (75mm Anti-tank Gun 40) Sd.Kfz. 234/4, it was decided to utilize the standard gun shield and carriage (minus its wheels) from the existing towed mount seen here and install it on the vehicle with only some very minor changes. *(Pierre-Olivier Buan)*

Pictured in a French museum is this German Second World War-vintage unarmoured half-track prime mover labelled the Light Towing Motor Vehicle 1-Ton Sd.Kfz. 10. It was also referred to as the 'D7'. Reflecting the usefulness of the platform, it was modified and eventually configured to serve in ten different variants, some of them both armed and armoured. *(Christophe Vallier)*

The first armoured version of the Light Towing Motor Vehicle 1-Ton Sd.Kfz. 10 appeared in German army service in 1940. It was referred to as the Light Armoured Observation Vehicle Sd.Kfz. 253 with an example pictured here. Because of the weight of the armoured body, its load-carrying capacity was less than that of the unarmoured Sd.Kfz. 10. The vehicle's designers omitted the first torsion bar and forward road wheels that appeared on the Sd.Kfz. 10. *(Patton Museum)*

The second armoured version of the Light Towing Motor Vehicle 1-Ton Sd.Kfz. 10 entered into German army service in 1941. Designated the Light Armoured Ammunition Carrier Sd.Kfz. 252, it was easily distinguished from the Light Armoured Observation Vehicle Sd.Kfz. 253 by its steeply-sloped rear armoured body that is evident in this photograph. (*Patton Museum*)

The most numerous of the armoured versions built upon the shortened chassis of the Light Towing Motor Vehicle 1-Ton Sd.Kfz. 10 was the Light Armoured Personnel Carrier Sd.Kfz. 250. A restored example is pictured here. The vehicle had a crew of two and carried four infantrymen. A total of 4,250 units of this design were built between June 1941 and October 1943. (*Bob Fleming*)

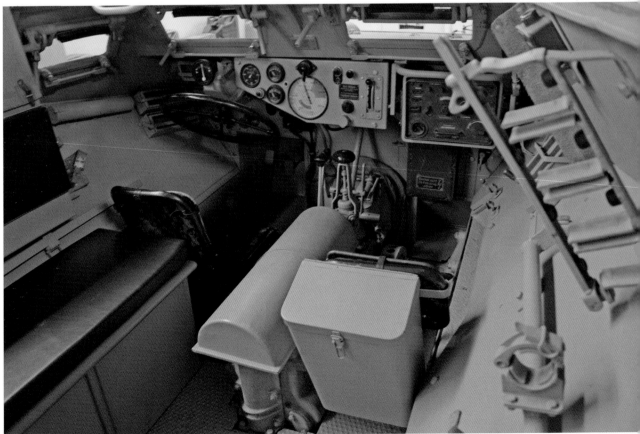

In the foreground is a four-man Light Armoured Radio Car Sd.Kfz. 250/3 fitted with rod antennas rather than the pre-war and early-war frame antennas. It was a multi-service vehicle employed by both German army reconnaissance units and by the German Air Force with a different radio to allow its forward air controllers to accompany German army motorized units. *(Patton Museum)*

(**Opposite, above**) Belonging to a British collector is this restored Light Armoured Personnel Carrier Sd.Kfz. 250. It weighs approximately 12,990lb. The vehicle length is 15ft with a width of 6ft 4in and a height of 5ft 4in. Top speed of the Sd.Kfz. 250 on level roads was 37mph with a maximum operational range of approximately 200 miles. *(Ian Wilcox)*

(**Opposite, below**) In this image we see the restored interior of the Light Armoured Personnel Carrier Sd.Kfz. 250 shown in the previous photograph. The first units of the vehicle were not delivered to the German army until the summer of 1941. The thickest armour on the open-topped Sd.Kfz. 250 was its front hull at 14.5mm. The sides and rear of the vehicle's armoured body were only 8mm thick. *(Ian Wilcox)*

(**Above**) Perhaps the most famous variant of the Light Armoured Personnel Carrier Sd.Kfz. 250 family of vehicles was the Light Armoured Observation Vehicle Sd.Kfz. 250/5. It is seen here employed by General Erwin Rommel during the fighting in North Africa in 1942. It was the replacement for the Light Armoured Observation Vehicle Sd.Kfz. 253 and came in two versions with different radio configurations. (*Patton Museum*)

(**Opposite, above**) On display at a French museum is this preserved example of a Light Armoured Car (20mm) Sd.Kfz. 250/9. Missing from its open-topped turret is the standard 20mm automatic gun and coaxial machine gun. This vehicle was the Eastern Front replacement for the 4 × 4 Light Armoured Car Sd.Kfz. 222 in 1943 due to its superior off-road capabilities. (*Christophe Vallier*)

(**Opposite, below**) The four-man Light Armoured Personnel Carrier (37mm Anti-tank Gun) Sd.Kfz. 250/10 pictured here had authorized stowage for 216 rounds of 37mm ammunition and 1,100 rounds for its non-coaxial machine gun. The 37mm gun fired an armour-piercing (AP) projectile with a muzzle velocity of 2,444 f/s and could penetrate 34mm of armour sloped at 30 degrees from the vertical at 1,094 yards. (*Patton Museum*)

2358g. 42

(**Opposite, above**) A partial replacement for the Sd.Kfz. 250/10 armed with a 37mm main gun was the Light Armoured Personnel Carrier (Heavy Anti-tank Gun 41) Sd.Kfz. 250/11 shown here. It was armed with a 28mm squeeze-bore gun that fired a tungsten AP projectile with a muzzle velocity of 4,691 f/s and could penetrate 60mm of armour sloped at 30 degrees from the vertical at 1,094 yards. (*Patton Museum*)

(**Opposite, below**) To speed up production and reduce costs a simplified version of the Light Armoured Personnel Carrier Sd.Kfz. 250/1 came off the factory floor in 1943. It differed only in the construction of its armoured body that went from having nineteen main plates to only nine. This resulted in a more box-like appearance as seen here in this preserved example. The only change to its designation was the addition of the word 'New'. (*Christophe Vallier*)

(**Above**) In the foreground of this picture is a burning Light Armoured Personnel Carrier Sd.Kfz. 250/1 (New). Behind it is a Light Armoured Personnel Carrier Sd.Kfz. 250/1 (Old), as is evident in the more complex shape of the front of the vehicle's armoured body. The Sd.Kfz. 250/1 (New) was modified to serve as the platform for almost all the variants of the Sd.Kfz. 250/1 (Old). (*Patton Museum*)

(**Opposite, above**) The preferred gun-armed version of the Sd.Kfz. 250 series that began coming off the production line until 1943 was the Light Armoured Personnel Carrier (75mm) seen here. It weighed approximately 14,100lb and had authorized stowage for twenty rounds of 75mm ammunition. It was the replacement for the Light Armoured Personnel Carrier (Heavy Anti-tank Gun 41) Sd.Kfz. 250/11 armed with the squeeze-bore 28mm anti-tank gun. (*Patton Museum*)

(**Opposite, below**) Adopted by the Waffen SS were a small number of 8 × 8 Austrian army armoured cars, one of which is seen here. They were labelled the Armoured Reconnaissance Vehicle ADGZ. Armed with a 20mm gun and two machine guns, they weighed approximately 26,890lb. The six-man vehicles were 20ft in length, had a width of 7ft 1in and a height of 8ft 4in. (*Patton Museum*)

(**Above**) With its successful defeat of the French army in the summer of 1940, the German army acquired a large stockpile of French army vehicles. This included the 4 × 4 Panhard 178 armed with a 25mm gun and a coaxial machine gun. In German army service the gasoline-engine-powered vehicle seen here was referred to as the Armoured Reconnaissance Vehicle Panhard 178-P204(f). (*Patton Museum*)

Pictured here is a unit of Hungarian army 4 × 4 reconnaissance armoured cars designated the 39M Csaba. It fought alongside its Axis counterparts during the early stages of the war on the Eastern Front. Introduced into Hungarian army service in 1939, the three-man gasoline-engine vehicle was armed with a 20mm automatic gun and a coaxial machine gun. *(Patton Museum)*

The Italian army had a shortage of armoured cars early in the Second World War. One stop-gap mounted the body of a First World War armoured car on a modern commercial 4 × 4 truck chassis. The resulting vehicle was called the FIAT-Terni Tripoli, with two knocked-out examples seen in this picture. *(Tank Museum)*

Shown here on patrol is a unit of Italian army reconnaissance 4 × 4 armoured cars designated the AB41. The four-man gasoline-engine-powered vehicle was armed with a 20mm anti-tank gun and two machine guns. One of the machine guns was a coaxial and the other was mounted in the armoured body to fire over the rear of the engine compartment. (*Tank Museum*)

The AB41 pictured here was the most numerous armoured car employed by the Italian army during the Second World War. The vehicle's turret was a modified version of that designed for the Italian L6/40 light tank. The AB41 weighed approximately 16,00lb, had a length of 17ft 1in, a width of 6ft 3in and a height of 8ft. (*Tank Museum*)

The planned Italian army replacement for the AB41 was the AB43, a restored example of which is seen here. It retained the armoured body of its predecessor but was fitted with a more powerful gasoline-powered engine and a new larger, roomier turret. Armament of the AB43 was the same as the AB41 with a 20mm anti-tank gun and two machine guns. (*Christophe Vallier*)

Based upon the 4 × 4 chassis of an unarmoured prime mover, the Italian army acquired 150 units of an open-topped armoured personnel carrier. It was designated the S37 and had a driver and up to eight passengers. At some point either one or two units were fitted with a turret armed with a 20mm anti-tank gun as seen here and labelled the North African Armoured Car TL37. (*Tank Museum*)

Very impressed by captured examples of the British army 4 × 4 Daimler Dingo armoured car, the Italian army commissioned a copy as seen here. It was named the 'Lynx' but entered into production too late for service with the Italian army. Rather it was taken into German army service in 1943 as the Armoured Reconnaissance Vehicle Lynx 202(i). It was also employed by Germany's allies. *(Christophe Vallier)*

Prior to the Second World War the Japanese navy bought a dozen British-designed and built 4 × 4 armoured cars referred to as the Crossley Indian Pattern Armoured Car for its naval infantry landing force. An example is seen here in China. The Japanese referred to it as the Type 97. The machine-gun-armed vehicle had a length of 16ft 6in, a width of 6ft and a height of 8ft 8in. *(Patton Museum)*

A Japanese-designed and built armoured car that entered into service in 1932 is the Model 92 Osaka shown here. Armed with two machine guns, the gasoline-engine-powered vehicle had a crew of three men. Maximum armour thickness on the armoured car was 8mm. It weighed approximately 12,800lb, had a length of 16ft 5in, a height of 8ft 8in and a width of 6ft 1in. (*Tank Museum*)

In 1933, the Japanese army introduced into service the Type 93 Sumida Armoured Car seen here. The machine-gun-armed vehicle could also be configured to ride on railroad tracks. With a gasoline-powered engine, top speed on level roads of the six-man armoured car was 37mph. It weighed approximately 15,400lb and was 21ft 6in in length with a width of 6ft 3in and a height of 9ft 8in. (*Tank Museum*)

Chapter Two

Assault Guns

In June 1936, the German army tasked industry to develop a suitable armoured tracked vehicle for the support of its infantry formations. It was to be turretless and mount a forward-firing gun 75mm or larger, capable of dealing with enemy defensive positions as well as the enemy tanks of its day. Its armour protection had to be able to stop 20mm AP projectiles on the front of the vehicle and machine-gun bullets on its sides and rear.

The original design guidelines called for the proposed new infantry support vehicle to be open-topped. It was later decided that an armoured roof was needed. Testing of five prototypes of the new infantry support vehicle built in 1937 went well and it was ordered into production in 1939. The first examples were rolling off the assembly lines in early 1940 and were labelled assault guns, which in German translates to *Sturmgeschütz*, abbreviated to StuG.

The majority of the assault guns built for the German army between 1940 and 1943 used the powertrain and suspension system of the Panzer III medium tank series. The hulls of the assault guns were similar to that of its tank counterpart but more thickly armoured. Due to production delays, a small number of assault guns were built upon the standard Panzer III chassis.

Assault Gun Models A–E

The German army employed a variety of names and designations for its assault guns that were sometimes changed. For the sake of brevity, the author will use what he considers the most commonly-employed names and designations. The first five models of the assault gun were labelled from A through to E and all had the same inventory number, Sd.Kfz. 142. In German these would be the following:

StuG Ausf. A (30 built)   StuG Ausf. D (150 built)
StuG Ausf. B (320 built)   StuG Ausf. E (272 built)
StuG Ausf. C (50 built)

'Ausf.' is the German abbreviation for the word *Ausführung* (model/version) with the letter following representing a design change to the vehicle in alphabetical sequence and denotes its production order in the series.

Weaponry

These first five models of the assault gun were all armed with the same short-barrel, low-velocity 75mm gun designated the 7.5cm StuK 37 (L/24). This was a derivative of the same gun mounted on the early-production models of the Panzer IV medium tank series.

The most common round for these weapons would be HE, which is not optimized for penetrating armour. For dealing with enemy tanks the assault guns were also provided with three types of short-range anti-tank rounds. These included an AP round, a HEAT round and – typically in very small numbers – a tungsten-core round designated the GrPatr38 HB/B.

In a US War Department Military Intelligence Service Information Bulletin dated May 1943 appears this extract describing the majority of ammunition types and their performance for the short-barrel 75mm gun mounted in the first five versions of the StuG series:

> For HE shells, the gun is sighted to 6,550 yards, for AP, only 1,640. At 500 yards, the penetration is 1.81 inches in 30 degree sloping armor, and 2.16 inches in vertical; at 1,200, it drops to 1.57 and 1.89 inches. The HE shell weighs 12.6 pounds; the AP stated shell, with cap and ballistic cap [APC], 14.81. There is an AP hollow charge [HEAT] of unstated weight, as well as a 13.56-pound smoke shell. In the bins of the carrier, 44 rounds are carried, and about 40 more may be stacked on the floor. A dozen stick grenades (potato mashers) may also be carried on a clip.

None of the first five assault gun models was fitted with a coaxial machine gun. The fifth model of the assault gun series was authorized a single machine gun stored within the vehicle. However, there was no mount or armoured shield on the roof of the vehicle for firing the weapon, the assumption being that the accompanying infantry would provide any suppressive fire needed.

Crew Positions

The assault gun crew consisted of a vehicle commander, gunner, loader and driver. The loader was on the right-hand side of the 75mm gun breech and the vehicle commander, gunner and driver on the left-hand side located one behind the other. The crews of the German army assault guns came from the artillery branch and were not tankers.

The vehicle commander, gunner and loader all had their own overhead hatches in the vehicle superstructure roof. The vehicle commander was provided with a scissor-type periscope, with the uppermost portion projecting out of his overhead hatch.

The assault gun driver entered the vehicle by way of the gunner's overhead hatch. An emergency exit path – in theory for the driver – was by way of the two-piece horizontal final drive access hatch in the front hull. It was located in front of him and below his position.

The driver had a direct-vision laminated glass block in the vehicle's front super-structure protected by a movable armoured flap. If that had to be closed, he could observe the outside world by means of a twin periscope (with two holes drilled into the front armoured superstructure plate) located directly above the armoured flap. There was also a direct-vision slit protected by laminated glass on the left front superstructure for the driver.

On the first two models of the assault gun, the gunner – who was located directly behind and above the driver in the vehicle's superstructure – had his internal pano-ramic periscope gunsight protected by an armoured visor in the front superstructure plate.

Beginning with the third model of the assault gun, the gunner's gunsight opening in the front superstructure was omitted. The gunner now relied on a single-lens pano-ramic periscope gunsight that projected out of a small opening in his overhead hatch. On all six early models of the assault gun series the gunner's periscope sight allowed for either direct or indirect fire.

Protection

Armour thickness of the first five models of the assault gun series was 50mm on the front superstructure and front hull. On the sides and rear of the vehicle's super-structure and hull the armour was 30mm thick; on the superstructure roof it was 11mm thick. The bottom of the vehicle's hull was 16mm thick.

In the September 1942 issue of the Military Intelligence Service Bulletin appears this extract referencing the protection on a StuG Ausf. D captured in North Africa: 'The sides of the hull are reported to be vulnerable to the British 40-mm antitank gun at 1,500 yards, but the gun can penetrate the front only at very close range, and even then only the driving compartment.'

Next-Generation Assault Guns

During the invasion of the Soviet Union in the summer of 1941, German tank and anti-tank guns had great difficulty in destroying the well-armoured T-34 medium and KV series heavy tanks of the Red Army at other than very short ranges. Hitler therefore ordered in September 1941 an up-armoured assault gun armed with a more powerful long-barrel 75mm gun labelled the StuK 40 (L/43) as a stop-gap measure. This new gun was intended to allow for the engagement and destruction of Red Army tanks at longer ranges.

The assault gun fitted with the long-barrel 75mm gun would be the sixth model in the series and labelled the StuG Ausf. F. This vehicle and follow-on versions would be assigned the inventory number Sd.Kfz. 142/1. A total of 359 units of the StuG Ausf. F

Assault Gun Employment

From a February 1943 issue of the Military Intelligence Service Bulletin appear these passages describing the assault gun tactical roles based on captured early-war German documents:

Support for the infantry in the attack is the chief mission of the assault gun by virtue of its armor, maneuverability, and cross-country performance and of the rapidity with which it can open fire. The moral support which the infantry receives through its presence is important.

It does not fire on the move. In close fighting, it is vulnerable because its sides are light and it is open-topped. Besides, it has facilities for defending itself at close quarters. As it is not in a position to carry out independent reconnaissance and fighting tasks, this weapon must always be supported by infantry.

In support of an infantry attack, the assault gun engages the enemy heavy infantry weapons which cannot be quickly or effectively destroyed by other weapons. In support of a tank attack, it takes over part of the role of the Pz.Kw. 4, and deals with enemy antitank guns appearing on the front. It will only infrequently be employed as divisional artillery [indirect fire] ... Its employment for its principal tasks must always be assured.

Assault guns are only to be used in towns and woods in conjunction with particularly strong and close infantry support, unless the visibility and field of fire are so limited as to make use of the gun impossible without endangering friendly troops. Assault guns are not suitable for use in darkness. Their use in snow is also restricted, as they must usually keep to available roads where enemy defense is sure to be met.

would be constructed between March and September 1942. The vehicle itself was a modified version of the previous StuG Ausf. E that was armed with the short-barrel 75mm gun.

Despite its new role as a back-up tank destroyer, a 1944 German army assault gun commander handbook reminded its readers of the following: 'Assault guns are employed according to artillery principles and should be regarded as first line artillery ... In every action the destruction of the enemy's tanks is a consideration of the utmost importance. Nonetheless, you must not permit your assault guns to be employed solely as tank destroyers.'

The StuG Ausf. F had a new gun mount and gun shield for the larger and heavier 75mm gun as well as a thickened front superstructure. To deal with the gaseous residue generated by larger rounds with more propellant being fired, a large electrically-powered exhaust fan was placed in the superstructure roof. Authorized main gun ammunition storage was fifty-four rounds on the StuG Ausf. F.

Upgraded StuG Ausf. F

In September 1942, the first units of an improved StuG Ausf. F came off the assembly line with an even longer-barrel 75mm gun labelled the StuK 40 (L/48). The vehicle was designated as the StuG Ausf. F/8. Its hull design differed from earlier assault guns as it was based on a later-production model of the Panzer III medium tank.

Some of the new design features of the StuG Ausf. F included larger engine air intakes and a 50mm thick rear hull plate. Some were provided with an armoured shield on the superstructure roof from which the loader could mount a machine gun carried on board the vehicle. By the time production of the StuG Ausf. F/8 concluded in December 1942, a total of 334 units had been built.

Final Model Based on the Panzer III

The last version of the assault gun series armed with a long-barrel 75mm StuK 40 (L/40) main gun and based on the chassis of the Panzer III medium tank was the StuG Ausf. G. It was redesignated in December 1943 as the StuG III Ausf. G. A total of 7,892 units of the StuG III Ausf. G would be constructed between December 1942 and March 1945.

During the long production run of the StuG III Ausf. G a great many design changes took place and some were more evident than others. These included the addition of a cupola with eight periscopes for the vehicle commander. In addition, the superstructure was made wider than on previous models.

The electrically-powered exhaust fan that had first appeared on the superstructure roof of the StuG Ausf. F was moved to the rear face of the superstructure on the

StuG III Ausf. G. Beginning in 1944, an opening for a coaxial machine gun was created for the two different types of gun shields fitted on the StuG III Ausf. G.

Early-production units of the StuG III Ausf. G were provided with an armoured shield in front of the loader's overhead hatch for the onboard stored machine gun. In 1944, it was replaced on the vehicle with a roof-mounted remote-control machine gun and a close-in-defence anti-personnel grenade-launcher.

Assault Gun Howitzer

As early as 1941 the German army had tasked industry with arming the existing assault gun with a 105mm howitzer. The first prototype appeared in early 1942. It was followed by nine pre-production units in October 1942. To test their combat effectiveness, in November 1942 they were shipped to a German army unit fighting the Red Army.

Positive field results with the 105mm-armed pre-production assault guns, labelled the 10.5cm StuH42 (L/28), resulted in a production contract being awarded. The vehicle was eventually labelled the Assault Howitzer 42 and assigned the inventory number Sd.Kfz. 142/2. The first production examples rolled off the assembly lines in March 1943. By the time production ended in February 1945, a total of 1,211 units had been completed.

Due to the larger calibre of its main armament, authorized stowage on the Assault Howitzer 105mm was limited to thirty-six rounds, divided between HE and HEAT. The 105mm howitzer was originally fitted with a muzzle brake that was omitted on later-production units.

Assault Guns on the Panzer IV Chassis

In early 1943, it was proposed that the superstructure of the existing StuG III Ausf. G, based on the Panzer III chassis, should be adapted to be fitted onto the Panzer IV chassis. This hybrid concept was initially rejected. On 26 November 1943 the main factory producing the StuG III Ausf. G was heavily damaged in a bombing raid.

To make up for the resulting production shortages, the idea of mating a StuG III Ausf. G superstructure to a Panzer IV chassis won approval in December 1943. The ensuing hybrid vehicle became the StuG IV Sd.Kfz. 167. A total of 1,139 came off the factory floor between December 1943 and March 1945. Some were diverted to tank destroyer units.

The grafting of the superstructure originally developed for a Panzer III onto the longer chassis of a Panzer IV resulted in some design changes. A new box-like armoured cab for the driver that extended out from the original superstructure was created. Like the StuG III Ausf. G, the new assault gun, based on the Panzer IV, was eventually fitted with a roof-mounted remote-control machine gun and a close-in-defence anti-personnel grenade-launcher.

The StuG Ausf. F was originally armed with a 7.5cm StuK 40 (L/43) gun that had a length of 10ft 9in. It was replaced by the 7.5cm StuK 40 (L/48) that was 12ft in length. By increasing the length of a gun barrel, higher muzzle velocities can be obtained, which in turn improves the performance of AP rounds.

Italian Assault Guns

The Italian army was impressed by the German army assault guns employed during the invasion of France in 1940. This resulted in the Italian army taking into service in 1941 their version of a turretless assault gun. It was labelled the Self-Propelled Gun 75/18, which in Italian is *Semovente da* 75/18. The number 75 in the designation represented the diameter of the weapon's bore, which was 75mm, and the number 18 the length of the barrel in calibres.

The Italian army assault gun was originally armed with a relatively short-barrel 75mm forward-firing gun. Unlike the German army that saw the primary role of their early-war assault guns as direct-fire infantry support vehicles, the Italian army initially placed their new assault gun into the indirect artillery fire role. As the Self-Propelled Gun 75/18 proved better-armed and armoured than the Italian army medium tanks on which it was based, plans were made to replace all the existing medium tanks with the superior assault guns.

In a US War Department Military Intelligence Service Information Bulletin dated May 1943 appears this extract on the short-barrel 75mm gun mounted in the Self-Propelled Gun 75/18:

> The gun has a traverse of 45 degrees and an elevation of from 15 degrees minus to 25 degrees plus. It is an 18-caliber weapon with a maximum range of 8,350 yards. The ammunition consists of 13.9-pound HE shell, 14.1-pound AP and a 14.5-pound shrapnel. Storage for only 29 rounds is provided, but many more will certainly be carried.

The call soon came from the Italian army for a longer-barrel 75mm armament on their assault gun. A prototype referred to as the Self-Propelled Gun 75/34 appeared in March 1943. Production began in May of that year but only sixty units were completed before the Italian government surrendered in September 1943. Between the Self-Propelled Gun 75/18 and the Self-Propelled Gun 75/34, approximately 300 units were built between 1941 and 1943.

New Ownership

With the Italian surrender, all their assault guns within the German army area of control in the country were seized, totalling 123 units. The Germans then had the factory that had made them for the Italian army restart the production line and built an additional fifty-five units between 1943 and 1945. The German army designated the Self-Propelled Gun 75/18 as the M42 75/18 850(i) and the Self-Propelled Gun 75/34 as the M42 75/34 851(i).

As had the German army, the Italian army eventually identified a requirement for an assault gun armed with a 105mm howitzer. This resulted in ninety-one units of the turretless Self-Propelled Gun 105/25 being constructed between 1943 and 1944. Upon Italy's surrender, the German army took into its inventory twenty-six units and had the Italian factory responsible for their construction build at least sixty additional units. In German army service the vehicle received the designation M43 105/25(i).

(**Below**) Shown here is a late-production StuG Ausf. B. It can be identified by the six-hole front drive sprocket. This design feature denotes it as having wider track than the earlier StuG Ausf. A. Whereas the StuG Ausf. A had a preselect transmission, the StuG Ausf. B came with a more advanced synchromesh transmission. (*Patton Museum*)

(**Opposite, above**) The crewmen of a StuG B are shown here loading their vehicle. There was authorized stowage on the vehicle for a total of forty-four rounds. Thirty-two were located directly in front of the loader's position and the other twelve were stored in a metal container on the interior rear wall of the vehicle. Also stored inside the vehicle were two submachine guns. (*Patton Museum*)

(**Opposite, below**) On this StuG Ausf. B the aperture for the gunner's internal optical sight has been hidden by an armoured flap. The bottom portion of the cut-out was ribbed to deflect bullets and other small battlefield fragments from being channelled into the gunner's internal optical sight when its protective flap was opened. (*Patton Museum*)

7·5 cm Sturmgeschütz

(75-MM ASSAULT GUN)

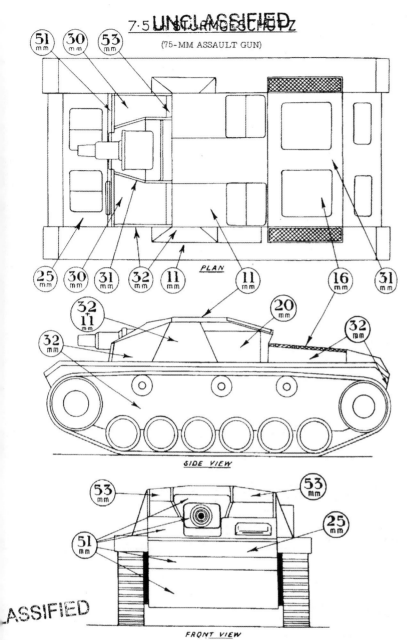

From an American War Department publication appears this line drawing of an early-model StuG Ausf. D with the armour thickness listed. The Western Allies seemed to be unaware that the armour on the early-model assault guns was thicker than that on the early-model Panzer III medium tank series. Armour on the latter was only 30mm thick on their front hull and superstructure. (*Patton Museum*)

PLAN

SIDE VIEW

FRONT VIEW

(**Opposite, above**) The deep cut-out in the upper superstructure on the Ausf. A and Ausf. B models of the StuG series proved to be a shot trap (re-entrant angle). This was somewhat corrected on the subsequent versions with a redesign of the upper superstructure as seen on this restored StuG Ausf. D. The gunner was now provided with a single-lens optical periscope that protruded through his overhead hatch. (*Ian Wilcox*)

(**Opposite, below**) On this restored StuG Ausf. D we can see that the front track roller has been moved forward on the hull. This identifies the vehicle as having the 1ft 4in-wide tracks that began appearing on the late-production StuG Ausf. B. Unlike the early-model Panzer III medium tanks, none of the assault guns had the side hull escape hatches seen on the former. (*Ian Wilcox*)

The scissor-type stereoscopic periscope pictured here was standard equipment on all variants of the StuG and had a fairly wide view of field. It was employed by the vehicle commander to identify targets and their range for the gunner who had a single-lens periscope with a relatively narrow field of view. It was typically the vehicle commander that directed the gunner's fire. *(Ian Wilcox)*

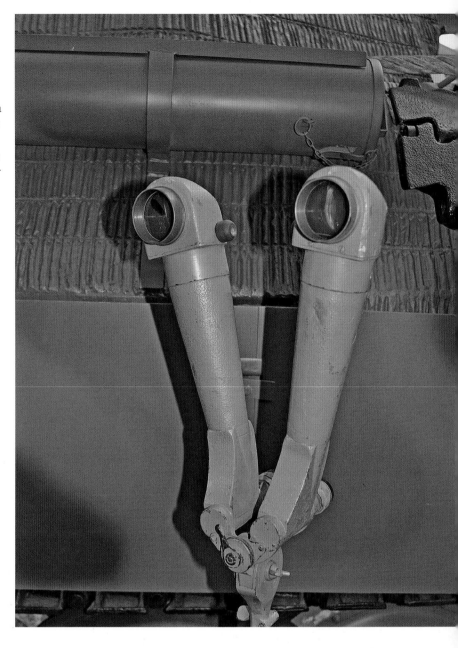

(**Opposite, above**) In this photograph we are looking downwards at a scissor-type stereoscopic periscope installed at the vehicle commander's position on a restored StuG Ausf. D. Visible under the device is the stand upon which it is affixed. The stand is attached to the left-hand side of the vehicle's interior superstructure wall next to the vehicle commander's position. *(Ian Wilcox)*

(**Opposite, below**) In this picture of a StuG Ausf. D we can see sunshades to reduce glare on the scissor-type stereoscopic periscope. On the forward side of the vehicle's superstructure we can see an angled plate placed there as spaced armour. It was 9mm thick. To the right of the angled spaced armour is an armoured sponson containing the vehicle's radio equipment. *(Patton Museum)*

(**Opposite, above**) On this restored StuG Ausf. D we can see the driver's direct-vision laminated glass block. Above that are the two holes for his direct-view binocular vision device. To the left of the driver's position is the bracket for the fitting of a rubber pad over a direct-vision port protected by laminated glass. The driver had no overhead hatch. (*Ian Wilcox*)

(**Opposite, below**) In this close-up view of a restored StuG Ausf. D we can see the two-piece final drive inspection hatches. Above and directly behind the open inspection hatches is the horizontal shot deflector in front of the driver's direct-vision laminated glass block. Additional protection for the laminated glass block is provided by the pivoting armoured cover directly above it. (*Ian Wilcox*)

(**Above**) The StuG Ausf. E seen here was very similar to the previous model but differed in some minor super-structure details. One was the elimination of the thin, angled, spaced armour plates on either side of the superstructure. On either side of the front glacis plate of the vehicle pictured are the vertical blackout covers for the headlights and below them the original design for the towing shackles. (*Patton Museum*)

13268
9.3.42.

13269
9.3.42.

(**Opposite, above**) In response to the threat posed by the Red Army T-34 medium tanks and KV heavy tanks, the German army rushed into service the StuG Ausf. F armed with a more potent long-barrel 75mm gun. A prominent design feature of this model was the large electrically-powered exhaust fan mounted in the rear of the raised superstructure roof. The uppermost portion is visible on the vehicle pictured here. (*Patton Museum*)

(**Opposite, below**) Unlike the short-barrel 75mm gun on the StuG Ausf. A through to Ausf. E that had its two recoil cylinders located on opposite sides of the weapon and protected by the 50mm thick gun shield, the new long-barrel 75mm gun on the StuG Ausf. F had its recoil cylinders located on top of the weapon. This resulted in a new wedge-shaped 50mm-thick gun shield as seen on this StuG Ausf. F. (*Patton Museum*)

(**Above**) On this StuG Ausf. F and seen on other examples of the vehicle is a layer of concrete added to the sloping front plates of the superstructure on the driver's side of the gun. This provided a better ballistic shape to these plates and avoided the shot trap (re-entrant angle) created by the vertical rear face at the rear of the sloping front plates of the superstructure. (*Patton Museum*)

(**Above**) The StuG Ausf. F shown here had at some point extra armour plates welded onto the front hull and superstructure. Sometime during production of the StuG Ausf. F the slope of the upper superstructure front plates on either side of the gun was increased. This almost completely eliminated the vertical shot trap (re-entrant angle) seen on previous assault guns. (*Patton Museum*)

(**Opposite, above**) To improve the tank-killing ability of the StuG Ausf. F, an improved model was introduced into service relatively quickly. It was armed with an even longer-barrel 75mm gun. The vehicle was assigned the designation StuG Ausf. F/8. It was also up-armoured with extra 30mm-thick plates bolted onto the existing 50mm base armour on both the hull (as seen in this photograph) and front superstructure. (*Patton Museum*)

(**Opposite, below**) The hull design of the StuG Ausf. F/8 pictured here was based on a modified version of the later-model production Panzer III Ausf. L medium tank. This resulted in a revised rear engine compartment that was longer and more thickly armoured than on previous assault guns. Some of the StuG Ausf. F/8 units were based on the hull and chassis of redundant Panzer III medium tanks. (*Patton Museum*)

(**Opposite, above**) The last version of the 75mm gun-armed StuG series based on the powertrain and suspension components of the Panzer III medium tank series was the StuG Ausf. G seen here. The vehicle designation was later changed to the StuG III Ausf. G. It was armed with the same long-barrel 75mm gun as the previous StuG Ausf. F/8 and based on the same chassis. (*Richard Hunnicutt*)

(**Opposite, below**) A noticeable design change to the StuG III Ausf. G was the vehicle commander's cupola seen here in this US army picture of a captured example. In front of the vehicle commander's cupola is the out-of-place gunner's overhead hatch with the small opening for his single-lens sighting periscope. Visible in its stowed position is the machine-gun shield for the loader. (*Patton Museum*)

(**Above**) The armour-protected roof-mounted electrically-powered exhaust fan of the StuG Ausf. F and F/8 was moved to the rear face of the superstructure as seen here on this restored StuG III Ausf. G. The loader's machine-gun shield has been erected in this picture. The orientation of the five cast-armour engine ventilator covers seen here on the roof of the engine compartment first appeared on the StuG Ausf. F/8. (*Bob Fleming*)

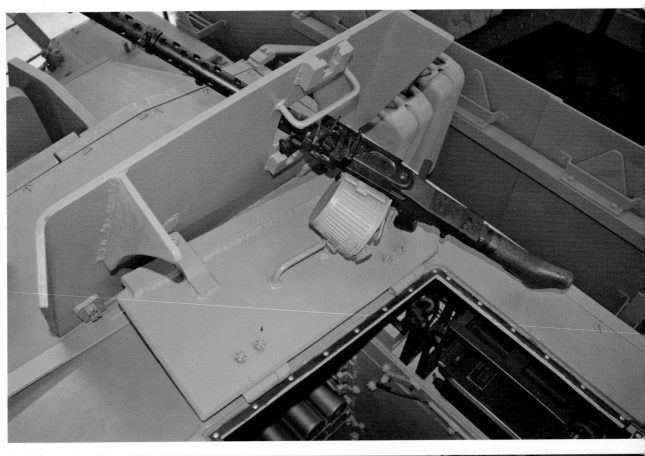

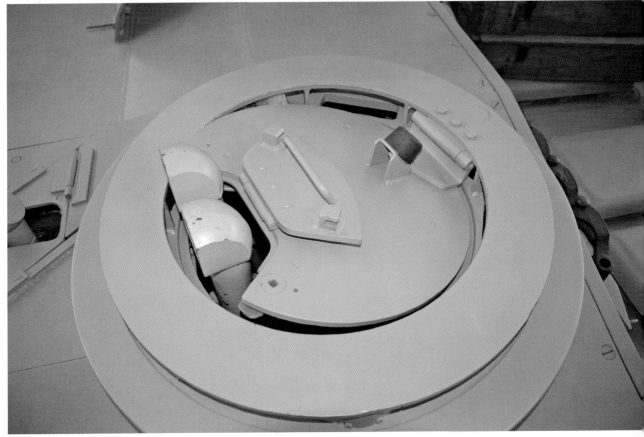

(**Opposite, above**) A close-up picture of the loader's machine-gun shield on a restored StuG III Ausf. G. Combat experience showed that it was not thick enough to protect the loader from the projectiles fired by the Red Army 14.5mm anti-tank rifles. This eventually led to the adoption of a remote-control machine-gun mount on the superstructure roof, from which the loader could aim and fire within the vehicle. (*Chris Hughes*)

(**Opposite, below**) An overhead view of the vehicle commander's cupola on a restored StuG III Ausf. G. Arranged around the circumference of the cupola would be eight periscopes. The small flap at the front of the overhead hatch allowed the vehicle commander to use his scissor-type stereoscopic periscope without the need to open the hatch if facing an overhead threat from artillery or mortar fire, for example. (*Chris Hughes*)

(**Above**) On display here is a preserved early-to-mid-production StuG III Ausf. G. This is indicated by the 30mm-thick plates bolted onto the existing 50mm-thick armour on the front hull and superstructure of the vehicle. Beginning in May 1943, new-built units of the StuG III Ausf. G left the factory with 80mm-thick base armour on their front hull. (*Thomas Anderson*)

(**Opposite, above**) For whatever reason two US army soldiers are shown working on the final drive of one of two captured examples of the StuG III Ausf. G. Both vehicles have the 80mm-thick front hull plates that began appearing on the production lines in May 1943. They retain the 50mm front superstructure base plates with the bolted-on 30mm extra plates. (*Patton Museum*)

(**Opposite, below**) On display at a Swiss museum is a preserved StuG III Ausf. G. The long-barrel 75mm gun on the vehicle seems to be partially retracted into the cylinder-like sleeve that forms part of the weapon's gun shield. The superstructure of the StuG III Ausf. G was slightly taller than its predecessors and wider. (*Andreas Kirchhoff*)

(**Above**) Between 1943 and 1944, the Finnish army bought fifty-nine units of the StuG III Ausf. G from the Germans. This preserved vehicle has been painted in a Finnish army camouflage scheme and markings from the Second World War. The Romanian army bought ninety-eight StuG III Ausf. G units from the Germans in 1943 and the Bulgarians were supplied with twenty-five units of the same vehicle by the Germans in the same year. (*Frank Schulz*)

In the approximate middle of the upper rear armour plate of this preserved StuG III Ausf. G is the circular armoured cover for the inertial crank starter. Below the upper rear armour plate is a curved sheet metal deflector to prevent dust being disturbed by the engine's cooling fans. The metal bracket fitted around the engine roof deck was for containing stowage items. *(Christophe Vallier)*

The vehicle commander of a StuG III Ausf. G is shown looking through his scissor-type stereoscopic periscope. Directly behind him is a submachine gun and ammunition pouch stored on the rear superstructure wall. Below those items is the interior portion of the electrically-powered exhaust fan that vents the gaseous residue generated when the gun's breech block opens upon recoil. *(Patton Museum)*

In this photograph we see the interior portion of the gunner's single-lens optical sighting instrument on a restored StuG III Ausf. G. It was designated the SflZF1a. Reflecting its origins as a self-propelled artillery piece, the gunner's sight could be employed in the direct fire or indirect fire modes. (*Chris Hughes*)

Looking downwards at the gunner's overhead hatch, located directly in front of the vehicle commander's cupola on a StuG III Ausf. G is the opening for the uppermost portion of the gunner's single-lens periscope that projected over the superstructure roof. Note that the gunner could use a sliding armour shutter to close the opening in his overhead hatch. (*Frank Schultz*)

Combat experience with the StuG III Ausf. G showed that the vehicle commander's raised cupola on the vehicle was more vulnerable to enemy fire than anticipated. Some crews attached spare track links around the base of the cupola for additional production. The factory solution applied to some vehicles involved welding a large piece of cast armour to the front of the vehicle commander's cupola as seen in this photograph. (*Patton Museum*)

Behind the loader holding an AP round in a StuG III Ausf. G is a stored submachine gun. Authorized main gun ammunition stowage on the vehicle was fifty-four rounds. Of those, some were in a ready-rack in the superstructure to the loader's right. There were additional rounds stored in racks on the hull floor directly in front of him. (*Patton Museum*)

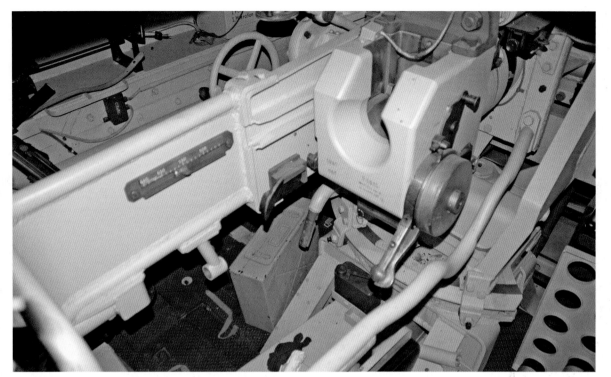

In looking down through the loader's hatch on a restored StuG III Ausf. G we can see the breech of the 75mm main gun. The metal tubing extending outward from the rear of the gun is the recoil guard. To the bottom right-hand side of the picture can be seen a portion of one of the vehicle's main gun ammunition racks on the hull floor fitted with dummy display rounds. *(Chris Hughes)*

The driver's station on a restored StuG III Ausf. G. To the right covered by the grey sheet-metal housing is the vehicle's transmission, which provided the driver with six forward gears and one reverse. Above the transmission is the driver's instrument panel. Top speed of the StuG III Ausf. G was 25mph on level roads. The operational range was approximately 100 miles. *(Chris Hughes)*

(**Opposite, above**) The spaced armour plates seen on this restored StuG III Ausf. G were intended solely for defence against the AP projectiles fired by Red Army 14.5mm anti-tank rifles. The two radio antennas at the rear of the vehicle's superstructure mark it as a command vehicle. Note the standard German army blackout light directly below the main gun on the front glacis plate. (*Author's collection*)

(**Above**) Here the 75mm main gun of a StuG III Ausf. G is being lowered into place by a crane. An American War Department publication dated May 1943 lists the AP projectiles fired by the gun as being able to penetrate 3.5in of sloped armour at 500 yards and 4.25in of vertical armour. At 2,000 yards, it is listed as being able to penetrate 2.44in of sloped armour and 3.03in of vertical armour. (*Patton Museum*)

(**Opposite, below**) Beginning in November 1943, some units of the StuG III Ausf. G were produced with the new cast-armour gun shield, seen here. It was referred to by the crews as the boar's head mount. Visible on this vehicle are the all-steel track support rollers that also began appearing in late 1943. (*Andreas Kirchhoff*)

(**Opposite, above**) Starting in June 1944 the 50mm-thick near-vertical superstructure plate on the right-hand side of the gun (normally fitted with a bolted-on 30mm supplemental armour plate) was replaced. In its place, there appeared an 80mm base armour plate as seen on this preserved StuG III Ausf. G. The 30mm bolted-on supplemental armour plate around the driver's visor was continued with until production ceased. (*Patton Museum*)

(**Above**) This restored StuG III Ausf. G has been covered with a reproduction of one version of the wartime anti-magnetic cement. The vehicle is 22ft in length, has a width of 9ft 7in and is 7ft 2in in height. The approximate loaded weight of the StuG III Ausf. G was 57,000lb. The visible front drive sprocket was a single-piece casting. (*Andreas Kirchhoff*)

(**Opposite, below**) Posed here with a number of re-enactors is a restored StuG III Ausf. G with anti-magnetic cement and the cast-armour gun shield. This particular vehicle features a layer of concrete over the superstructure plate over the driver and gunner's position. Note that this StuG III Ausf. G also has the cast-armour shot deflector welded to the vehicle commander's cupola. (*Tank Museum*)

(**Opposite, above**) This unrestored StuG III Ausf. G, which is missing its vehicle commander's cupola, was pulled from a bog in Latvia. The original machine-gun shield for the loader survived and is folded down on the roof of the superstructure. Despite the introduction of the cast-armour gun shield visible on this vehicle, the welded-armour gun shield remained in production until the end of the war. (*Author's collection*)

(**Above**) Pictured here is an unrestored StuG III Ausf. G. A design feature that disappeared with the introduction of this model of the assault gun was the two holes for the driver's binocular vision device. An interesting design feature of the vehicle commander's cupola on the StuG III Ausf. G was the fact that its uppermost portion could be rotated through 360 degrees. (*Thomas Anderson*)

(**Opposite, below**) Note on the visible superstructure side of this StuG III Ausf. G that the crew has stacked a number of track links vertically for additional protection. The crew has also erected a line of vertically-arranged track links at the rear of the engine compartment roof to hold items stored on the engine deck, which includes spare road wheels. (*Patton Museum*)

(**Opposite, above**) Shown here with American stars added is a captured StuG III Ausf. G. Note that the entire forward superstructure roof has been covered with a thick layer of concrete by its former owners. Also note that the shield-protected remote-control mount located above the loader's position is armed with an MP44 Assault Rifle instead of the standard machine gun. (*Patton Museum*)

(**Opposite, below**) On display at an Israeli museum is this StuG III Ausf. G. It had been captured from the Syrian army during the 1967 Arab-Israeli conflict. The Syrian army had acquired a number of German army tanks and AFVs from the Second World War in the 1960s. The bracket over the gun shield and the gun shield in front of the vehicle commander's cupola are Syrian additions. (*Vladimir Yakubov*)

(**Above**) On the way to the front is this StuG III Ausf. G. Note that a track link has been attached to the front vertical plate on the loader's side of the vehicle's superstructure. Such was the importance of increasing the armour protection on the StuG III Ausf. G that the German army informed the manufacturers that a decrease in the vehicle's mobility was acceptable. (*Patton Museum*)

(**Opposite, above**) Seen here on display at the now-closed Patton Museum of Armor and Cavalry is this StuG III Ausf. G in its original camouflage paint scheme. On the right-hand side of the cast-armour gun shield is an opening for a coaxial machine gun, which began appearing on late-production units of the vehicle. The eight periscopes in the vehicle commander's cupola could be raised and lowered independently. (*Author's collection*)

(**Opposite, below**) Eventually the need arose for a more powerfully-armed version of the StuG III Ausf. G optimized for the infantry support role. This led to the production of a variant armed with a 105mm howitzer, a preserved example of which is seen here. It was labelled the 105mm Assault Howitzer Sd.Kfz. 142/2. (*Richard Hunnicutt*)

(**Above**) On display at a French museum is a preserved example of a 105mm Assault Howitzer Sd.Kfz. 142/2. The muzzle brake on this particular vehicle is not correct. Due to the larger weapon and correspondingly larger ammunition, the vehicle was restricted to authorized stowage of only thirty-six main gun rounds. (*Christophe Vallier*)

(**Above**) It was eventually decided that the 105mm Assault Howitzer Sd.Kfz. 142/2 did not require a muzzle brake to operate effectively. This led to its being deleted from the production line, as seen on this preserved example. Besides the standard HE rounds, the vehicle would typically have carried some HEAT rounds for taking on enemy tanks. (*Dean and Nancy Kleffman*)

(**Opposite, above**) Later-production units of the 105mm Assault Howitzer Sd.Kfz. 142/2 were equipped with a large cast-armour gun shield as seen in this wartime photograph. The 105mm howitzer with which it was armed was a version of the same weapon mounted on a German army self-propelled howitzer named the *Wespe* (Wasp). (*Patton Museum*)

(**Opposite, below**) German officers are shown on the rear engine deck of a StuG IV during a firing exercise. The vehicle consists of the modified superstructure of a StuG III Ausf. G grafted onto the chassis of a Panzer IV medium tank. As the chassis of the Panzer IV was longer than the superstructure of the StuG III Ausf. G, a new box-like driver's station extended forward from the superstructure as seen in this photograph. (*Patton Museum*)

A preserved StuG IV in a Polish museum. The front of the vehicle's superstructure was 80mm thick. The four-man vehicle weighed approximately 51,500lb. It had a length of 21ft 10in, a width of 9ft 7in and a height of 7ft 2in. On level roads the StuG IV had a top speed of 24mph and a maximum range of 130 miles. (*Pierre-Olivier Buan*)

An American soldier is looking over what is left of a StuG IV identified by the extended driver station with the open hatch. One could surmise that the vehicle had become bogged down and was destroyed by its crew before departing using a demolition charge normally carried on board all German tanks and AFVs. (*Patton Museum*)

The Italian army counterpart to the German assault guns was the Self-Propelled Gun 75/18. Pictured here is a restored example in a French museum. Armed with a short-barrel 75mm howitzer with a pepper-pot muzzle brake, there was authorized stowage on board for a total of forty-four main gun rounds. It was also armed with one or two machine guns. (*Christophe Vallier*)

The three-man Self-Propelled Gun 75/18 seen here weighed approximately 29,000lb. It was 16ft 1.5in long, had a width of 7ft 6in and a height of 6ft 1in. Top speed on level roads was 19mph, with a maximum operational range of 130 miles with its diesel-powered engine that produced 125hp. (*Patton Museum*)

(**Above**) Pictured here are a number of Self-Propelled Gun 75/18 units that had been seized by the German army from the Italian army upon the latter country's surrender to the Western Allies in September 1943. The armour on the near-vertical face of the vehicle's superstructure was 25mm thick. The gun shield was 50mm thick and the front hull had a thickness of 30mm. (*Patton Museum*)

(**Opposite, above**) As with the German army, the Italian army was forced into up-gunning its assault gun. This was accomplished by arming the existing Self-Propelled Gun 75/18 with a long-barrel 75mm gun optimized for firing AP rounds. The first production example did not leave the factory until April 1943 and, as Italy surrendered just five months later, most of those built served with the German army. (*Patton Museum*)

(**Opposite, below**) The Royal Hungarian Army fielded sixty-seven units of an assault gun during the Second World War armed with a short-barrel 105mm howitzer. A knocked-out example is seen here in the foreground. It was named the *Zrinyi* II. There were plans for the production of a *Zrinyi* I armed with a long-barrel 76mm anti-tank gun but Hungary was knocked out of the war before production could begin. (*Patton Museum*)

Chapter Three

Tank Destroyers

As early as 1934 there were some within the German army that had begun thinking about the requirement for a dedicated tank destroyer. This led to the building of a number of armoured half-track prototypes armed with turreted and non-turreted 37mm or 75mm anti-tank guns. The testing of these prototypes did not lead to any production contracts being awarded.

Shortly before the German invasion of Poland in September 1939, the German army once again began exploring the concept of a tank destroyer based on a half-track with a secondary role as a bunker-buster. Eventually, a third role as an anti-aircraft vehicle was envisioned. The chassis chosen for this role were two different-sized unarmoured half-track prime movers: the Sd.Kfz. 8 and the Sd.Kfz. 9.

For their new role both half-tracks were lightly armoured and armed with a shield-protected 88mm anti-aircraft gun labelled in German as the FlaK 18 L/56. Production commenced in 1939 and continued until 1940 with a combined total of twenty-five being built. They would see use during the German invasions of Poland in 1939 and France and the Low Countries in 1940.

Full-Tracked Tank Hunters

Prior to the invasion of France in the summer of 1940 there had arisen some thought on the requirement for a full-tracked tank destroyer. In German, a tank destroyer can be referred to as a *Panzerjäger* (tank hunter) or as a *Jagdpanzer* (hunting tank). Unlike assault guns crewed by artillerymen, tank destroyers were crewed by tankers.

The need for a full-tracked tank destroyer led to the fielding between March 1940 and February 1941 of 202 units of the vehicle referred to as the 'Tank Hunter I'. It consisted of the obsolete chassis of the gasoline-engine-powered Panzer I light tank armed with a forward-firing Czech 47mm anti-tank gun protected by an open-topped superstructure. This vehicle never had an ordnance inventory number.

In a Military Intelligence Service Information Bulletin published in May 1943 appears this extract describing the arrangement and performance of the Czech 47mm anti-tank gun mounted in the Tank Hunter I:

> The Skoda gun has a 30-degree traverse with an elevation of from minus 8 degrees to plus 12. The AP tracer shell, 3.68 pounds, has a velocity of 2,540 f/s,

penetrating at 300 yards 2.32 inches of armor at 30 degrees, and 2.99 inches at normal angle [vertical]. At 1,000 yards the respective penetrations are 1.85 and 2.44 inches. An HE shell of 5.07 pounds and an AP 40 of 1.81 pounds are used. The effective range is not stated, but is apparently 1,000 yards. About 74 rounds are carried.

The Tank Hunter I would see its combat debut during the French campaign. Thereafter, it would go on to see action in a variety of theatres, including the German invasion of the Balkans and the Soviet Union in 1941. Unable to deal with the Red Army T-34 medium tank and the KV series heavy tanks, it was eventually pulled from service in 1943.

In December 1940, the German army decided that the captured French army Renault R35 light tanks would be a better choice as the platform for the Czech 47mm anti-tank gun than the Panzer I. This resulted in the construction between May and October 1941 of 174 units of the German army's second improvised tank destroyer. It was labelled the 47mm Anti-tank Gun (Czech-built) tank 35R (French-built) on a captured tank chassis.

Design Dead-Ends

In late 1940, the German army asked industry for a self-propelled vehicle armed with a weapon capable of destroying heavily-fortified enemy bunkers. In response, industry came up with two identical prototypes for Hitler's inspection in March 1941. They were based on the chassis of a Panzer IV and armed with a 105mm gun mounted in a forward-firing position. The gun crew was protected by an armoured superstructure.

By May 1941, the proposed bunker-busting vehicle was being considered for the role of a heavy tank hunter. It became Self-propelled Gun on Tank Chassis IV. However, by early 1942 this idea was dropped and the vehicle was never ordered into production. In spite of this, both prototypes were sent to the Eastern Front for combat trials, one being destroyed in combat and the other eventually returned to Germany.

A second larger proposed heavy tank hunter appeared in early 1942. It was armed with a forward-firing 128mm gun mounted on the chassis of an experimental gasoline-engine-powered heavy tank designated the VK3001 (H). Only two prototypes were built and both were sent to the Eastern Front for combat trials. It was never ordered into production.

From a November 1943 Military Intelligence Service Bulletin appears this passage regarding the Western Allies' awareness of the 128mm gun-armed vehicle and their take on its discerned purpose:

It is believed that the '128' may be used for the most part against fixed fortifications, in which case protection would be supplied by other means, which is further indicated by the fact that no machine gun is reported as part of the equipment. Only 18 rounds of separate-loading ammunition are carried. While the type of shell is not yet reported, mixed AP and anti-concrete may be expected. The crew is five.

The Shock of Combat

The German army entered into the Second World War in 1939 with the belief that its medium tanks – the Panzer III and IV – possessed sufficient firepower to deal with the majority of enemy tanks likely to be encountered on near-term battlefields. However, its faith was badly shaken during the invasion of France in 1940 when some of its opponent's tanks proved to be more heavily-armoured than anticipated and therefore extremely difficult to destroy.

Before the German army ordnance department could rectify the firepower shortcomings of its medium tanks, Hitler ordered the invasion of the Soviet Union in 1941. Much to everybody's dismay, once again the firepower of the German medium tanks came up short when confronted with the Red Army's new T-34 medium tank and KV heavy tank series.

Because the newest generation of Red Army tanks were still limited in numbers in 1941 and also badly-employed, the superior training and tactics of the German tankers generally allowed them to prevail on the battlefield. There was, however, no illusion that this advantage would last very long. The short-term solution was to field as many improvised tank destroyers as quickly as possible with the most powerful guns available.

A Stand-In Gun

During the initial stages of the German invasion of the Soviet Union a large number of Red Army towed 76.2mm field/anti-tank guns were captured. As there was a shortage of German-designed and built towed 75mm anti-tank guns at the time, it was decided to re-chamber the Red Army 76.2mm anti-tank gun to fire German 75mm anti-tank ammunition. It then became the 7.62mm PaK 36(r), the (r) signifying that the gun was Russian-built.

From a May 1943 US War Department Military Intelligence Service Bulletin appears this passage regarding the performance of the 7.62mm PaK 36(r):

The 7.62-mm Russian field gun Model 36 (7.62cm PaK 36(r)) with a long, thin barrel throws a 14.8-pound capped armor-piercing shell at the relatively low velocity of 2,200 f/s [feet per second], a 14-pound HE at 2,340 f/s, and an AP 40 shot [tungsten carbide-core] of 9.25 pounds weight at 2,800 f/s.

The 7.62mm PaK 36(r) was mounted on the chassis of both the Panzer II light tank and the Panzer 38(t) light tank. The (t) in the latter vehicle's designation meant that it was Czech-built. Both vehicles were considered obsolete at that time by the German army.

There were three versions of the Panzer II series light tanks on which were mounted the 7.62mm PaK 36(r). These included the E, D and F models. All of them were listed as the Sd.Kfz. 132, with a total of 201 units completed between April and June 1942. Most served on the Eastern Front until all were pulled from front-line service in early 1944.

The prototype for the first-generation tank hunter based on the chassis of the Panzer 38(t) and armed with the 7.62mm PaK 36(r) appeared in December 1941. Production began in April 1942 and was completed sometime in 1943 with a total of 353 units built. It was listed as the Sd.Kfz. 139 and was also referred to as the Tank Hunter 38(t) as well as the 'Marder III'. Almost all served on the Eastern Front with a number being sent to fight with the German army in North Africa.

Sometime in late 1941 nine units of the half-track prime mover Sd.Kfz. 6 were armed with the 7.62mm PaK 36(r). The gun crew was protected by a tall open-topped armoured superstructure. All nine examples were employed by the German army fighting in North Africa and were subsequently lost.

The Romanian army also made use of captured Red Army towed 76.2mm anti-tank guns. In the first case, they mounted the weapon on the chassis of captured Red Army T-60 light tanks and labelled it the TACAM T-60. Only thirty-four units were constructed in 1943.

The Romanian army also converted twenty units of their Czech-designed and built R-2 light tank to mount a re-chambered Red Army 7.62mm anti-tank gun. They were assigned the designation R-2 TACAM and protected by a thinly-armoured open-topped superstructure, as was the TACAM T-60.

The Preferred Gun

The German army counterpart to the 7.62mm PaK 36(r) was designated the 7.5cm PaK 40 (L/46). The German 75mm gun had a higher muzzle velocity than its Soviet-built counterpart of 3,248 f/s and fired an armour-piercing capped (APC) projectile. This meant that it offered greater armour penetration capabilities.

The APC projectile of the 7.62mm PaK 36(r) could penetrate 82mm of armour sloped at 30 degrees at a range of 1,094 yards. An APC projectile fired from the 7.5cm PaK 40 (L/46) was able to punch a hole through 97mm of armour sloped at 30 degrees at the same distance.

As soon as production of the German 7.5cm PaK 40/3 (L/46) reached sufficient levels, it was mounted on the Panzer II chassis and listed as the Sd.Kfz. 131. The three-man tank destroyer was also known by the name 'Marder II'. It was built between June 1942 and March 1944 with a total of 651 units constructed.

The German 7.5cm PaK 40 (L/46) gun was also mounted on the gasoline-engine-powered Panzer 38(t) light tank chassis and listed as the Sd.Kfz. 138. Making matters a bit confusing, the Sd.Kfz. 138 came in two different configurations. The first version was built upon the chassis of the Panzer 38(t) Ausf. H, and the second on the chassis of the Panzer 38(t) Ausf. M.

A total of 417 units of the Sd.Kfz. 138 were built between November 1942 and sometime in 1943 on the chassis of the Panzer 38(t) Ausf. H. There were 973 units of the Sd.Kfz. 138 completed between April 1943 and May 1944 on the Panzer 38(t) Ausf. M chassis. It was also referred to as the Marder III.

Didn't Work Out

In 1943, the German army approved the experimental conversion of an Austrian-designed and built full-tracked unarmoured prime mover into an armoured tank destroyer. The original vehicle and the experimental tank destroyer were intended for use only on the Eastern Front. It was labelled the Self-propelled Anti-tank Gun on a Tracked Truck Chassis.

The Austrian full-tracked unarmoured prime mover was known as the *Raupenschlepper Ost* (Caterpillar Tractor East) or 'RSO' for short. For the proposed tank destroyer role, it was armed with a German 75mm anti-tank gun PaK 40 (L/46) mounted on a 360-degree turntable. Other than the weapon's gun shield, the only other armour protected the driver's cab. Sixty pre-production units were sent to the Eastern Front for combat trials in early 1944. However, no series production contract was awarded for the vehicle.

French Sideshow

In 1942, it was decided by the German army to modify three French-designed armoured vehicles into improvised tank destroyers by arming them with the German 75mm PaK 40 (L/46). None were intended for service on the Eastern Front but only for the then inactive Western Front.

One of the three vehicles – an armoured logistical support vehicle – was known as the Lorraine 37L. The other two were based on the chassis of pre-war light tanks built by Hotchkiss and Renault; the former was the H39 and the latter the FCM36. A total of 170 units of the Lorraine 37L and 24 units of the H39 were converted into tank destroyers in 1942. Ten units of the FCM36 were converted into tank destroyers in 1943.

Another Improvised Tank Hunter

The most potent anti-tank gun in the German army inventory was the 8.8cm PaK 43 (L/71). By late 1941, the German army had already decided that they wanted the gun mounted on either the Panzer III or Panzer IV tank chassis. As the design constraints of both vehicles made that impossible, German industry came up with a specialized chassis for mounting the 8.8cm PaK 43 (L/71). It was a hybrid of components from both medium tanks and assigned the designation *Geschützwagen* (Gun Carriage) III/IV.

The vehicle was originally assigned the nickname 'Hornisse' (Hornet), later changed to 'Nashorn' (Rhinoceros) by Hitler's order in February 1944. Both were listed as the Sd.Kfz. 164. A total of 494 were produced between February 1943 and March 1945 in two slightly different versions. They would see action on both the Eastern Front and against the Western Allies.

Not Letting Anything Go to Waste

In the course of development of the Tiger E (Tiger I) heavy tank, Hitler had expressed his desire to see it armed with the 8.8cm KwK 43 (L/71). Design constraints made that impossible, so the Tiger E was armed with an 88mm main gun designated the 8.8cm KwK 36 (L/56).

Still wanting to field a well-armoured vehicle armed with the 8.8cm KwK 43 (L/71), it was decided in September 1942 that a new heavy assault gun armed with a version of the weapon designated the 8.8cm PaK 43 (L/71) be fielded. The vehicle chassis selected for mounting the gun were 90 of the 100 units of the rejected Tiger (P) heavy tank chassis, which had been commissioned by Dr Ferdinand Porsche.

Production of the gasoline-engine-powered vehicle labelled the 'Ferdinand' took place between April and May 1943. By the time it entered into service the Ferdinand was classified as the 'Tank Hunter Tiger P' or 'Heavy Tank Hunter'. Combat introduction of the Ferdinand occurred in the summer of 1943. From a report by Ferdinand platoon commander Boehm, dated 19 July 1943, appears the following extract:

> On the first day of action, we successfully engaged bunkers, infantry, field and anti-tank artillery positions. For three hours, our guns [vehicles] fought in the cavalcade of enemy fire and proved to be immune to enemy fire! In the evening of the first day, first enemy tanks were destroyed, while others retreated. Crews of field and anti-tank guns run away after firing a few ineffective shots against our guns. In the first engagements, our regiment destroyed numerous artillery positions, bunkers as well as 120 enemy tanks.

The battlefield effectiveness of the 88mm gun on the Ferdinand was offset by the vehicle's weight, which limited its off-road mobility. Serious mechanical reliability issues also affected the vehicle throughout its service career. Another design error was not fitting the Ferdinand with any secondary armament, leaving it exposed to enemy infantry tank-hunting teams when it outran its supporting units and was rendered immobile for whatever reason.

From a 1943 Red Army publication named *Red Star* appears this translated passage by Lieutenant Colonel of Engineers K. Andreev on his impressions of the Ferdinand on the battlefield:

The powerful gun [vehicle] has its faults which make it vulnerable for antitank agents. Its great overall weight and the insufficient power of its motors account for the lack of speed. Its maneuverability across terrain is limited. Getting stuck in ditches and along the sides of roads is a relatively frequent occurrence when used on the battlefield. One captured enemy soldier from a battalion of self-propelled Ferdinand guns revealed that four out of the company's nine weapons [vehicles] went out of action on the march because of technical failures.

In late 1943, the surviving fifty units of the Ferdinand were returned to Germany for rebuilding. As part of their rebuilding process they were fitted with a ball-mounted machine gun in the front glacis plate operated by the radioman. Other improvements included wider tracks to improve off-road mobility and the addition of a vehicle commander cupola originally designed for the StuG III Ausf. G.

From an article in a 1944 issue of *Red Star* titled 'Heavy Self-Propelled Guns in Tank Battles' authored by Lieutenant Colonel G. Khainatskii appears this extract:

There has been a continuous increase in the caliber of the self-propelled gun and the thickness of its armor [Ferdinand], and the very appearance of self-propelled guns in battle formations of tanks shows the tendency to increase the firepower of the armored formation as much as possible, even at the expense of its maneuverability as a whole (self-propelled guns are less maneuverable than tanks but are superior to them in firepower).

There are two reasons why the self-propelled gun is used in tank formations: first, to free the tanks from the necessity of dueling with antitank guns, tanks, and self-propelled guns of the enemy; and second, to enable the tanks to maneuver on the battlefield under favorable conditions. In this regard, the self-propelled gun may be compared to a shield protecting the tank maneuver.

In early 1944, forty-eight units of the Ferdinand, now renamed the *Elefant* (Elephant), were returned to combat. Some went to Italy and others returned to the Eastern Front. As before, their size and weight, compounded by the continued unreliability of their engines and powertrains, caused more losses to mechanical breakdowns than to combat action. They would continue to see service in ever-decreasing numbers until the war in Europe ended in May 1945.

Panzer IV-Based Vehicles

Referred to as a tank destroyer and assault gun by the German army was the *Jagdpanzer* IV (Hunter Tank IV) Sd.Kfz. 162. Armament was the same 75mm gun as fitted to the StuG III Ausf. G but mounted in a newly-designed superstructure fitted to a Panzer IV chassis. A total of 769 units were constructed between January and November 1944.

Considered under-gunned, the *Jagdpanzer* IV was replaced on the production lines in December 1944 by an up-gunned version designated the Panzer IV/70 (V) Sd.Kfz. 162/1. The 75mm main gun on the vehicle was labelled the 7.5cm PaK 42 (L/70). It was the same weapon as mounted in the Panther medium tank series in which it was designated the KwK 42 (L/70). Production of the Panzer IV/70 (V) Sd.Kfz. 162/1 began in August 1944 and continued until March 1945 with a total of 930 units constructed.

A third tank destroyer based on the Panzer IV medium tank chassis was designated the Panzer IV/70 (A). It consisted of a modified version of the upper superstructure from the Panzer IV/70 (V) Sd.Kfz. 162/1 grafted onto the lower superstructure of a standard Panzer IV Ausf. J medium tank. A total of 278 units were built between August 1944 and March 1945.

Panther Tank-Based Hunter Tank

The German army had expressed interest in an assault gun version of the yet-to-be-built Panther medium tank in August 1942. It was to be armed with the same 88mm gun as mounted in the Rhinoceros and the Ferdinand. Originally classified as an assault gun, by the time it entered into service it was being referred to as either the 'Hunting Panther' Sd.Kfz. 173 or 'Tank Hunter Panther' Sd.Kfz. 173.

Production of the Hunting Panther took place between January 1944 and March 1945 with approximately 415 units built. The initial plans called for 150 units to be built per month. However, Allied bomber raids on German industry and the country's transportation infrastructure made that number impossible to achieve. The highest number constructed in a single month was attained in January 1944, with seventy-two units coming off the assembly lines.

Vehicle Description and Employment

A British military report listed as Appendix J to War Office Technical Intelligence Summary No. 142, dated 6 September 1944, describes a captured Hunting Panther:

> The unit consists of a normal Panther chassis with a superimposed super-structure, which is virtually a Panther glacis plate and sides extended upward to form a spacious fighting compartment, with a sloping rear plate. A noticeable feature is the amount of room available in the fighting compartment to enable the gun to be easily serviced, and the fact that all the elaborate observation facilities are on the roof plate, there being no vision openings at the front or sides of the vehicle except for the driver's episcope periscope.

In a Hunting Panther, the British army found authorized stowage space for fifty-seven main gun rounds, twenty-eight AP and the remainder HE. In another example, they found authorized stowage for only forty-nine main gun rounds, with additional rounds being stored on the vehicle floor.

The driver of the vehicle was located on the left-hand side of the 88mm main gun that divided the vehicle's superstructure in half. Besides the standard intercom system, the vehicle commander located on the right-hand side of the main gun of the Hunting Panther could transmit his commands to the driver by a novel method described in a British army report:

> Apart from the usual controls associated with a normal Panther chassis there is a control resembling that of a ship's telegraph on the front offside of the fighting compartment for transmitting the commander's orders to the driver in the nearside front of the vehicle.
>
> The commands reverse left, reverse right, forward left, forward right and halt may be transmitted by moving a lever opposite the required order on the commander's side, when a pointer, accompanied by a clang of a bell, points to the corresponding order on a panel in front of the driver.

No doubt having learned their lesson from the Ferdinand, the German army fitted the Hunting Panther with a machine gun in a ball mount on the right-hand side of the glacis from the beginning. It was originally intended that the vehicle commander would operate the weapon. This was quickly seen to be a mistake and the radioman who had been positioned behind him in the initial crew seating arrangement switched locations with the vehicle commander. This meant that the radioman became responsible for operating the vehicle's machine gun.

New Light Tank Destroyer

In response to a production shortfall caused by the Allied bomber raid of 26 November 1943 that badly damaged the factory building the majority of the StuG III Ausf. G Sd.Kfz. 142/1, the German army and industry developed two solutions. The first, as already discussed, was to begin production of the StuG IV Sd.Kfz. 167. This involved the grafting of a modified superstructure of a StuG III Ausf. G onto the chassis of a Panzer IV medium tank.

However, the German army still lacked a sufficient number of assault guns, which by this time were primarily tank destroyers, to meet all its requirements. After exploring different options, it was decided to field a new light tank hunter. Once again, the obsolete but proven chassis of the Panzer 38(t) light tank was utilized.

Rather than the improvised arrangement of the first-generation tank destroyers with their main guns mounted on the existing superstructure of the vehicles and protected by open-topped, thinly-armoured arrangements, a specially-designed, low-slung reasonably well-armoured superstructure was fitted to a modified Panzer 38(t) light tank chassis. Armament was the 75mm main gun designated the 7.5cm PaK 39 (L/48), which lacked a muzzle brake.

Name Changes

The new light tank destroyer went through a series of designation changes during its short time in service with the German army. Initially it was the StuG 38(t). It then became the 'Tank Hunter 38' followed by 'Hunter Tank 38'. The inventory number Sd.Kfz. 138/2 remained the same throughout its service career. The vehicle also acquired the unofficial nickname *Hetzer* (small fast hunting dog) during its wartime service, which actually had been assigned to a prototype tank hunter never built.

Production of the *Hetzer* began in April 1944 and continued until the end of the war in Europe with a total of 2,787 units completed. The largest number built occurred in January 1945 with 434 units completed. The target goal set by the German army had been 500 units per month; however, Allied bombing raids made that number difficult to achieve.

The Romanian army had wanted to take the *Hetzer* into service but their request was denied. The Hungarian army's request was looked upon more favourably by the German army and seventy-five units were eventually provided to them.

The following German wartime report dated October 1944 describes the effectiveness of the *Hetzer* in combat:

> Light tank destroyer Jagdpanzer 38 [Hunter Tank 38] proved itself in combat. Crews are proud of them and they as well as the infantry have confidence in them. The most praised is the option of all-around fire from the [roof-mounted] machine gun. Great firepower, low profile and overall shape proved suitability to fulfill two main tasks: fighting enemy tanks and direct support of the infantry in defense and offense. It occurred that a single company in short time destroyed 20 enemy tanks without any losses. One unit destroyed 57 enemy tanks (including two Stalins [IS-2 heavy tanks] at 800m) without any losses. This same unit arrived in the combat area after traveling during the day the distance of 160km [99 miles] without any breakdowns… Frontal armor can withstand Soviet 76.2mm gun fire. Current losses are results of [the thinner] side and rear plates being hit.

Crew Positions

The *Hetzer* was far from the perfect design, with very poor ergonomics for its four-man crew. Originally it was planned that the vehicle commander and loader/radio operator would be on the right-hand side of the centrally-mounted main gun with the vehicle commander behind the loader/radioman, the driver and gunner on the left-hand side, with the gunner directly behind the driver.

Due to the cramped interior of the *Hetzer*, the main gun was eventually mounted on the far right-hand side of the fighting compartment. This pushed the loader to the left-hand side of the gun and its breech. Unfortunately, due to the rush to field the vehicle, the loader's gun safety switch and most of the main gun ammunition remained on the opposite side of his location. This made it extremely awkward for the loader to service the piece.

The Biggest Gun Possible

In February 1943, German industry was tasked with the development of a 'Hunting Tiger' to be armed with a 128mm gun. It was to be mounted on the lengthened chassis of a yet-to-be-built new heavy tank. A full-size wooden mock-up of the proposed new Hunting Tiger was displayed for Hitler's inspection in October 1943. Having received the German leader's blessing, the first prototype was completed in April 1944.

Production of the vehicle labelled the *Jagdtiger* (Hunting Tiger) Sd.Kfz. 186 did not begin until January 1944 and ended in March 1945. Besides the name Hunting Tiger, the gasoline-engine-powered vehicle also went by the following German designations: 'Hunting Tiger VI' and 'Tank Hunter Tiger'.

The original plans had called for the building of 150 units of the Hunting Tiger but only 85 were eventually completed. The first eleven production units featured a Porsche-designed suspension system that proved unable to deal with the vehicle's weight. This forced the switch to the same Henschel-designed suspension system used on the Tiger B heavy tank (Tiger II).

The introduction of the Hunting Tiger into the field by the German army was not impressive, as can be seen in this passage from the book *Tiger im Schlamm* (*Tigers in the Mud*) written by the famous German Tiger tank ace Otto Carius:

> When the assault guns [*Jagdtigers*] were calibrated in Sennelager [Germany], we experienced our first failure. Despite its 82 tons, our Hunting Tiger didn't want to act like we wanted it to. Only its armor was satisfactory, its maneuverability left a lot to be desired. In addition, it was an assault gun. There was no traversing turret, just an enclosed armored housing. Any large traversing of the main gun had to be done by moving the entire vehicle. Because of that, transmission and steering differentials soon broke down. That such a monstrosity had to be constructed in the final phase of the war made no sense at all.

Besides its extremely thick frontal armour, the other redeeming feature of the Hunting Tiger was its 128mm main gun designated the PaK 44 (L/55). Due to the 58lb weight of the 128mm rounds they were separate-loading; hence two loaders were required on the vehicle. At a range of 1,094 yards the weapon's standard AP projectile traveling at 2,821 f/s could penetrate 142mm of armour plate sloped at

30 degrees. With a range of 2,187 yards the AP projectile could still punch through 117mm of armour sloped at 30 degrees. This would allow it to successfully engage the Red Army IS-2 Stalin heavy tanks at its maximum range.

Italian Tank Destroyers

To increase the number of self-propelled tank destroyers for the Italian army, the Self-Propelled Gun 47/32 was placed into production. It consisted of the chassis of the *Carro Armato* or Armoured Vehicle L6/40 light tank fitted with an open-topped armoured superstructure into which a 47mm anti-tank gun was fitted.

Approximately 300 units of the Armoured Vehicle L6/40 were built between 1941 and 1943. When Italy surrendered to the Western Allies in September 1943, the German army impounded seventy-eight units and relabelled them the StuG L6 *mit* 47/32 770(i). These vehicles would remain in use until the end of the war in Europe.

As the Italian army was seeking a better-armed tank destroyer for the Eastern Front, Italian industry provided thirty units of the Self-Propelled Gun 90/53 in 1942. It consisted of the chassis of a medium tank armed with a shield-protected 90mm anti-aircraft gun. A US War Department Military Intelligence Service Information Bulletin published in June 1943 describes the vehicle's arrangement:

> On the basis of the present report, it appears that this gun is mounted on the rear of a turretless 14-ton, Model 14/41 tank chassis. In order to accommodate the gun, it would appear that the normal positions of the engine and trans-mission in the hull have been rearranged. The engine, normally in the rear, seems to have been moved forward to the center of the hull, access being provided by two doors in the superstructure roof. There is probably room for one member of the crew besides the driver in front of the engine. It would seem that the engine is overloaded, so that the vehicle is slower and less maneuverable than the M14/41 tank. Presumably the 125-hp diesel engine of the M14/41 tank is retained.

The same 90mm anti-aircraft gun on the Self-Propelled Gun 90/53 was also mounted on either a 4 x 4 or 6 x 6 heavy truck. A combined total of 120 units of these wheeled tank destroyers were built between 1941 and 1943 for the Italian army. In a Military Intelligence Service Information Bulletin published in May 1943 appears this extract describing the types of rounds and the performance of the truck-mounted Italian 90mm anti-aircraft gun:

> A muzzle velocity of 2,756 f/s gives the 22.2 pound HE shell a range of 19,100 yards. The practical rate of fire is from 15 to 20 rpm. The elevation is from slightly below horizontal to 85 degrees, and the traverse is 360. An AP shell

of unknown weight is reported to penetrate 4.41 inches of plate [armour] on a 30-degree slope at 500 yards, and 5.63 inches of plate at the vertical. At 2,000 yards, the respective penetrations are 3.15 and 4.13 inches.

Japanese Tank Destroyers

To deal with the American M4 series medium tanks first encountered by the Imperial Japanese Army in 1943, Japanese industry managed to put into very limited production two tank destroyers between 1944 and 1945. Both were based on the chassis of the Type 97 medium tank chassis. However, Japanese industry could not build more tank destroyers as it was overwhelmed by all the other requirements of its armed forces.

The two tank destroyers built were the Type 1 Ho-Ni I and the Type 3 Ho-Ni III. Both armed with the same 75mm field gun, the primary difference was in their respective armoured superstructures. The former – of which 124 units were built – had an open-topped three-sided armoured superstructure, and the latter – of which 41 were constructed – had a fully-enclosed armoured superstructure.

Pictured is a self-propelled version of the famous 88mm anti-aircraft gun mounted on a German army half-track. It appeared in service just before the Second World War. Ten units were constructed in 1939 as a tank destroyer, among other roles. The decision was then made to switch to a larger half-track to mount the same gun, of which fifteen were built in 1940. Both vehicles were lightly armoured. (Patton Museum)

The Tank Hunter I seen here consisted of the obsolete chassis of the Panzer I light tank fitted with a three-sided open-topped armoured superstructure housing a Czech 47mm anti-tank gun. The official designation for the Czech gun in German service was 4.7cm PaK(t) (L/43.4). The vehicle had a top speed on level roads of 25mph and an operational range of 87 miles. *(Patton Museum)*

The three-man Tank Hunter I seen here in North Africa weighed approximately 14,300lb. It was 14ft 5in long with a width of 6ft 8in and a height of 7ft 4in. There was authorized stowage space on the vehicle for eighty-eight rounds. The vehicle's front hull and superstructure had a maximum frontal armour thickness of 13mm and the gun shield 14.5mm. *(Patton Museum)*

When the German army decided that the Panzer I tank chassis was not up to the job as a tank destroyer, it chose to use the chassis of a captured French army light tank referred to as the R35 upon which to mount a Czech 47mm anti-tank gun in the typical open-topped superstructure. A preserved example of the three-man vehicle is seen here on display at a Swiss museum. (*Andreas Kirchhoff*)

A factory photograph of one of the two prototypes built in 1941 of a self-propelled 105mm howitzer mounted on a Panzer IV medium tank chassis. The vehicle was originally envisioned as a bunker-buster but was later considered for the role of tank destroyer. The open-topped superstructure was 30mm thick, while the front hull thickness was 50mm. (*Patton Museum*)

An artist's rendition of a German heavy tank destroyer armed with a 128mm gun that appeared in a wartime US army War Department publication. Only two prototypes of the vehicle depicted here were built in early 1942. It weighed 78,400lb and had a crew of five. Frontal armour on the chassis as well as the open-topped superstructure and gun shield was 50mm. (*Patton Museum*)

In the foreground is a German army tank destroyer based on the obsolete chassis of the Panzer II light tank listed as the Sd.Kfz. 132. It was armed with a captured Red Army 76.2mm towed anti-tank gun re-chambered to fire German 75mm ammunition. In German service the gun was designated the PaK 36 (L/51.5). The four-man vehicle had authorized stowage for thirty main gun rounds. (*Patton Museum*)

(**Above**) The four large road wheels and lack of return rollers on this Sd.Kfz. 132 mark it as being based on the chassis of either an Ausf. D or Ausf. E model of the Panzer II light tank series. A combined total of only forty-three units of the Panzer II Ausf. D and E were built. The bulk of the Sd.Kfz. 132 units armed with the re-chambered 76.2mm Red Army anti-tank gun were based on the chassis of the Panzer II Ausf. F light tank. (*Patton Museum*)

(**Opposite, above**) Pictured is a preserved Tank Hunter 38(t) Sd.Kfz. 139. It is shown here on display at the former US Army Ordnance Museum, which was located at Aberdeen Proving Ground in Maryland. Like the Panzer II-based tank destroyer Sd.Kfz. 132, it was armed with a captured Red Army 76.2mm towed anti-tank gun re-chambered to fire German 75mm ammunition. (*Christophe Vallier*)

(**Opposite, below**) On a North African battlefield is this knocked-out Tank Hunter 38(t) Sd.Kfz. 139 or tank hunter. The vehicle had a four-man crew and weighed approximately 23,900lb. It was 19ft 2in in length with a width of 7ft 1in and a height of 8ft 2in. The frontal armour on the Tank Hunter 38(t) hull and superstructure was 50mm thick and the gun shield only 11mm. (*Tank Museum*)

(**Above**) Housed in a French museum is this preserved Tank Hunter 38(t) Sd.Kfz. 139. There was authorized stowage on board for thirty main gun rounds. The crew was also issued a machine gun for self-defence. The vehicle's gasoline-powered engine provided it with a top speed on level roads of 26mph and an operational range of 115 miles. (*Christophe Vallier*)

(**Opposite, above**) A relatively unknown Axis tank destroyer is the Romanian army TACAM R-2 seen here. It consisted of the chassis of their R-2 light tank, which was of Czech design and construction, armed with a captured Red Army 76.2mm field/anti-tank gun re-chambered to fire Romanian 75mm ammunition. Twenty were constructed in 1943. The vehicle's armoured superstructure was made from armour plate cut off from captured Red Army tanks. (*Charles Kliment*)

(**Opposite, below**) Shown here on display at the now-closed Patton Museum of Armor and Cavalry is a preserved Marder II Sd.Kfz. 131. It was armed with a German 75mm anti-tank gun labelled the PaK 40/2 instead of the re-chambered Red Army 76.2mm anti-tank gun that was mounted in the Panzer II light tank-based tank destroyer Sd.Kfz. 132 or the Tank Hunter 3(t) Sd.Kfz. 139. (*Dean and Nancy Kleffman*)

(**Opposite, above**) The Marder II Sd.Kfz. 131 rode on the standard Panzer II light tank chassis as is evident from the road wheel and return roller arrangement of this preserved example. Note the large leaf springs. Only the limited-production Ausf. D and E models of the Panzer II light tank series had the four large road wheels on either side of the hull and lacked return rollers. (*Christophe Vallier*)

(**Opposite, below**) The Panzer 38(t) light tank chassis was reconfigured in 1942 to accommodate a German 75mm anti-tank gun labelled the PaK 40/3. It then became the Panzer 38(t) Ausf. H Sd.Kfz. 138 pictured here. It can be distinguished from the Marder III Sd.Kfz. 139, also based on the Panzer 38(t) light tank chassis, by a different super-structure arrangement. The four-man vehicle had authorized stowage for thirty-eight main gun rounds. (*Patton Museum*)

(**Above**) Upon reflecting on the design of the Panzer 38(t) Ausf. H Sd.Kfz. 138, industry soon came to the conclusion that it could be improved. This resulted in a fairly extensive remodelling of the vehicle with the engine being relocated to the middle of the hull and the gun moved to the rear. This new configuration was labelled the Panzer 38(t) Ausf. M Sd.Kfz. 138 with a restored example shown here. (*Christophe Vallier*)

(**Above**) Belonging to the US army museum system is this Panzer 38(t) Ausf. M Sd.Kfz. 138. It weighs approximately 10,600lb and is 16ft 2in in length. The vehicle width is 7ft with a height of 8ft 1in. On level roads the Panzer 38(t) Ausf. M Sd.Kfz. 138 had a top speed of 26mph and an operational range of 118 miles. (*Christophe Vallier*)

(**Opposite, above**) On display at a French museum is a preserved Panzer 38(t) Ausf. M Sd.Kfz. 138, also known as the Marder III. This was a name shared with the Tank Hunter 38(t) Sd.Kfz. 139. Both were based upon the modified chassis of the Panzer 38(t) light tank. Both the vehicle superstructure and front hull were 50mm thick but the gun shield was only 15mm. (*Christophe Vallier*)

(**Opposite, below**) In early 1944, a pre-production batch of an improvised tank destroyer was sent to the Eastern Front for combat trials. They consisted of an Austrian-designed and built full-tracked logistical support vehicle armed with a German 75mm anti-tank gun as seen here. Armour thickness on the driver's cab was only 5mm. The field trials must have not been positive as series production was never approved. (*Christophe Vallier*)

(**Opposite, above**) The Germans took captured French army armoured full-tracked logistical supply vehicles and turned them into improvised tank destroyers in 1942 as seen here. They were labelled as a Self-propelled Anti-tank Gun on Captured Tracked Carrier Chassis. Armament was a German 75mm anti-tank gun designated the PaK 40/1 (L/46) as seen here with this preserved example. The gun shield was only 10mm thick. (*Christophe Vallier*)

(**Above**) There appeared in 1942 an improvised tank destroyer armed with a German 75mm PaK 40 (L/46) anti-tank gun as shown here. Based on the H-39 French light tank, it was referred to as the 7.5cm PaK 40 (Sf) *auf Geschützwagen* 39H(f). This translates to 75mm anti-tank gun/self-propelled armoured vehicle/tank 39H/French. The front hull had a maximum thickness of 34mm with the gun shield being 20mm thick. (*Christophe Vallier*)

(**Opposite, below**) Seen here on display at the former US Army Ordnance Museum is a preserved *Nashorn* (Rhinoceros) armed with an 88mm anti-tank gun. Prior to February 1944, it was named the *Hornisse* (Hornet). It was based on a hybrid chassis composed of Panzer III and Panzer IV components and listed as the Sd.Kfz. 164. The vehicle had a crew of four. (*Author's collection*)

The Hornet/Rhinoceros seen here in an ambush position weighed approximately 53,700lb. It was 27ft 8in in length, had a width of 9ft 6in and a height of 8ft 8in. Top speed on level roads was 26mph with an operational range of 134 miles. The chassis hull had a frontal thickness of 30mm with the gun shield being only 10mm thick. (*Patton Museum*)

In its original configuration as pictured here the six-man Ferdinand tank destroyer lacked any secondary machine-gun armament or vehicle commander's cupola. The front superstructure of the vehicle was protected by armour 200mm thick. The upper and lower front hull was 100mm thick, with the sides and rear of the vehicle being 80mm. The superstructure roof was 50mm thick. (*Patton Museum*)

In September 1943, the forty-eight surviving units of the Ferdinand were returned to Germany for rebuilding. Part of this rebuilding involved adding a front-hull machine gun and a vehicle commander's cupola as seen on this preserved example captured in Italy by the US army. In May 1944, Hitler ordered that the Ferdinand be renamed the *Elefant* (Elephant). *(David Doyle)*

Pictured here is the towed version of the 88mm anti-tank gun mounted in the Ferdinand/*Elefant* designated the 8.8cm PaK 43/2 (L/71). At a range of 546 yards the weapon firing a standard armour-piercing capped (APC) projectile with a muzzle velocity of 2,237 f/s could penetrate 185mm of armour sloped at 30 degrees. At 1,093 yards it could punch through 165mm of armour sloped at 30 degrees. *(Christophe Vallier)*

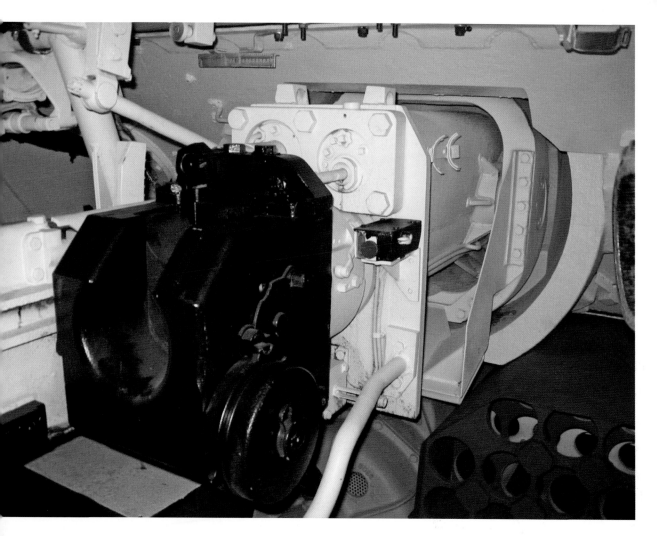

(**Opposite, above**) The mine-damaged *Elefant* pictured here weighed approximately 150,000lb and rode on a torsion-bar suspension system. It had a length of 26ft 7in, a width of 11ft 1in and a height of 9ft 7in. It was driven by two air-cooled gasoline engines that provided power to a single generator that in turn drove two electric motors attached to the two rear-hull-mounted drive sprockets. (*Patton Museum*)

(**Opposite, below**) The ballistic shape of the superstructure on the StuG IV was not optimum. Engineers soon came up with a redesigned superstructure for the vehicle with more sloping plates better able to deflect AP projectiles. That vehicle was designated the *Jagdpanzer* IV Sd.Kfz. 162 with a preserved example pictured here. It was armed with the same 75mm main gun as the StuG IV. (*Andreas Kirchhoff*)

(**Above**) The breech end of the 75mm main gun on a preserved *Jagdpanzer* IV. The vehicle had authorized stowage for 79 main gun rounds and 1,200 machine-gun rounds. Weighing in at approximately 56,000lb, the assault gun was 22ft 5in long, had a width of 10ft 4in and a height of 6ft 1in. Top speed on level roads was 25mph with a maximum range of 124 miles. (*Frank Schulz*)

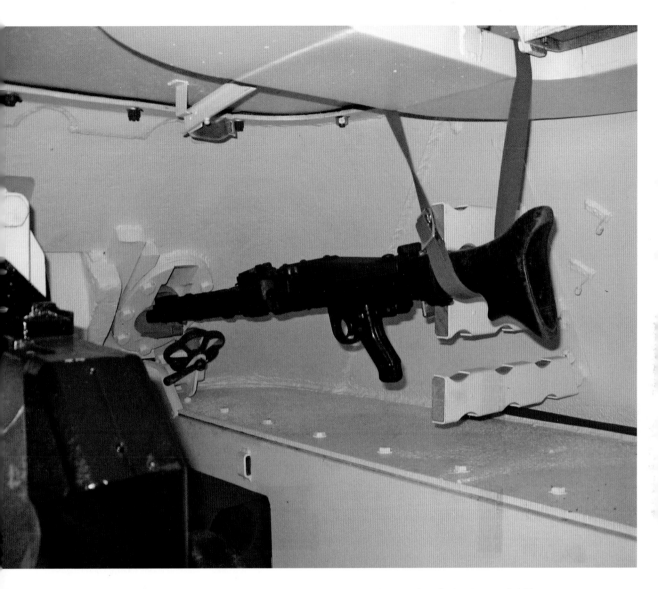

(**Opposite, above**) On display at a French museum is this preserved example of a *Jagdpanzer* IV. The cast-armour gun shield on the vehicle was 80mm thick. The front superstructure sloped at 30 degrees and the front hull sloped at 45 degrees were both originally 60mm thick. Side superstructure armour plates were sloped at 30 degrees and originally 30mm thick. (*Christophe Vallier*)

(**Opposite, below**) Residing in a German museum is this preserved *Jagdpanzer* IV. On the right-hand side of the front superstructure is a pivoting armour cap for an onboard machine gun. Very early-production examples had also had an armoured cap on the left-hand-side front superstructure for a second machine gun. Late-production units of the *Jagdpanzer* IV were fielded without a muzzle brake. (*Frank Schulz*)

(**Above**) In this picture we are looking at the machine gun on the right-hand side of a restored *Jagdpanzer* IV. The armour thickness on later-production units of the vehicle was increased on the front superstructure and upper hull from 60mm to 80mm. The superstructure sides of the *Jagdpanzer* IV went from 30mm to 40mm thick. (*Frank Schulz*)

(**Opposite, above**) On display at an Eastern European museum is this preserved Panzer IV/70 (V) listed as the Sd.Kfz. 162/1. It was an up-armed version of the *Jagdpanzer* IV Sd.Kfz. 162. The big difference was the addition of a longer-barrelled more powerful 75mm main gun, which lacked a muzzle brake. To support the longer barrel and heavier gun the vehicle was provided with a travel lock visible in this photograph. (*Thomas Anderson*)

(**Opposite, below**) Taking part in an historical military vehicle rally in Great Britain is this restored Panzer IV/70 (V) Sd.Kfz. 162/1. The armour on the upper front hull was 80mm thick and the lower portion of the front hull 50mm thick. The sloped front superstructure of the vehicle was 80mm and the sides 40mm. The height of the vehicle was 6ft. By way of comparison, the Panther medium tank was 9ft 9in tall. (*Bob Fleming*)

(**Above**) One might suspect that the Panzer IV/70 (V) Sd.Kfz. 162/1 pictured here drove by accident into this large shell crater and could not be recovered. It was therefore blown up by its crew. One feature that was specific to this vehicle and not its predecessor the *Jagdpanzer* IV Sd.Kfz. 162 was that the first three road wheels were steel-rimmed rather than rubber-rimmed. (*Patton Museum*)

(**Opposite, above**) Forming part of the extensive collection of Second World War vehicles belonging to the US army museum system is this preserved Panzer IV/70 (V) Sd.Kfz. 162/1. This particular example is missing the front hull travel lock. The vehicle main gun is being held up in position by two large blocks of wood visible in this picture. (*Richard Hunnicutt*)

(**Opposite, below**) Residing in a French museum is this battle-damaged Panzer IV/70 (A) Sd.Kfz. 162/1. In the upper glacis plate is an embedded AP projectile that failed to penetrate the 80mm-thick armour plate in that area. The sides of the upper structure are 40mm thick with the roof being 20mm. The superstructure roof was 20mm thick, as was the rear of the vehicle hull. (*Christophe Vallier*)

(**Above**) Either abandoned or knocked out is this Panzer IV/70 (A) Sd.Kfz. 162/1. The vehicle weighed approximately 62,700lb. By comparison the Panzer IV/70 (V) Sd.Kfz. 162/1 weighed about 57,800lb. The Panzer IV/70 (V) Sd.Kfz. 162/1 was 28ft long with a width of 9ft 4in and a height of 7ft 8in. Note that the four front road wheels are steel-rimmed. (*Patton Museum*)

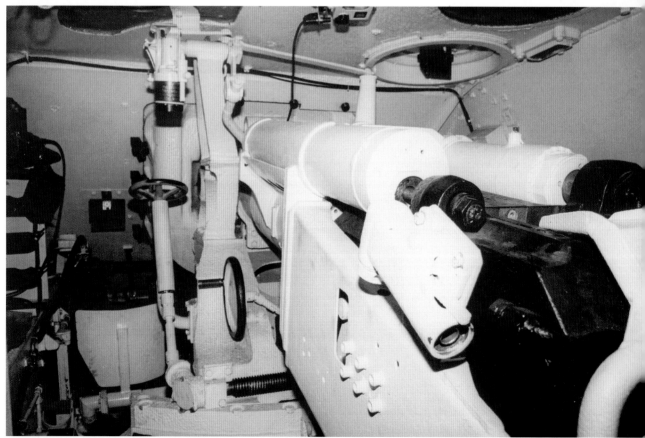

(**Opposite, above**) Belonging to a British museum is this preserved Hunting Panther Sd.Kfz. 173. The design of the armour collar around the 88mm main gun marks it as a pre-June 1944 production vehicle. The version pictured here was attached to the glacis by internal bolts and studs. (*Pierre-Olivier Buan*)

(**Above**) This pre-1944 production Hunting Panther Sd.Kfz. 173 forms part of the collection of a French museum. The 88mm main gun has a 100mm-thick cast-armour gun shield. The glacis was 80mm thick and the superstructure sides 50mm. Roof armour was only 13mm on the first fifty units, subsequently thickened to 30mm. The bottom of the vehicle's hull was also 30mm thick. (*Christophe Vallier*)

(**Opposite, below**) In this photograph we see the left-hand-side breech of the 88mm main gun on a restored Hunting Panther Sd.Kfz. 173. Visible on the top of the breech are the two long cylinders that comprise the vehicle's recoil system. On the lower left side of the breech are the gunner's manually-operated elevation and traverse handwheels. (*Andreas Kirchhoff*)

(**Opposite, above**) Beginning in June 1944, production Hunting Panther Sd.Kfz. 173 units received a new armoured recessed bracket. Rather than being held in place by internal bolts and studs as was the case with the original configuration, the new version seen here on a preserved example was larger and thicker and bolted to the glacis at both its top and bottom. (*Christophe Vallier*)

(**Above**) The driver of the Hunting Panther Sd.Kfz. 173 sat on the left-hand side of the 88mm main gun breech. His leather-cushioned seat is visible in this photograph taken inside a restored example. Directly in front of his seat can be seen his periscope mounted in the vehicle's glacis. If the periscope was damaged the driver could replace it without leaving the vehicle. (*Andreas Kirchhoff*)

(**Opposite, above**) The pre-June 1944 production units of the Hunting Panther Sd.Kfz. 173 had a muzzle brake that was 21in long and had a maximum diameter of 12in. It weighed 132lb. The post-June 1944 muzzle brake as seen here on this museum vehicle was 17in long with a maximum diameter of 9in and weighed 77lb. (*Tank Museum*)

(**Opposite, above**) At the rear centre of the superstructure roof of this restored Hunting Panther Sd.Kfz. 173 is the uppermost portion of the electrically-powered ventilation fan. On the left front side of this picture is the low-slung armoured protrusion from which the vehicle commander's scissor-type periscope protrudes. On the right front side is the roof opening for the gunner's periscope sight not seen here. (*Andreas Kirchhoff*)

(**Opposite, below**) This photograph shows the large rear superstructure hatch through which main gun rounds would be loaded into the Hunting Panther Sd.Kfz. 173. No doubt it would also be employed as an escape hatch when crewmen were forced to leave the vehicle while under fire from the front. To the right of the hatch can be seen the small circular hatch through which spent main gun cartridge cases would be ejected from the vehicle. (*Andreas Kirchhoff*)

(**Above**) In this picture of a restored Hunting Panther Sd.Kfz. 173 we are looking through the hatch located in the rear of the superstructure at the left-hand side of the 88mm main gun. At the rear of the breech is a fold-up panel that is lowered prior to firing the main gun and is employed by the loader to support the large and heavy main gun rounds prior to being inserted into the breech. (*Andreas Kirchhoff*)

(**Opposite, above**) Shown running is this restored late-production Hunting Panther Sd.Kfz. 173 belonging to the German military museum system. The vehicle has a top speed on level roads of 28mph and an operational range of 99 miles. The five-man vehicle weighs approximately 103,000lb. It is 22ft 9in long with a width of 10ft 9in and a height of 8ft 3in. (*Andreas Kirchhoff*)

(**Above**) The restored late-production Hunting Panther Sd.Kfz. 173 seen here belongs to a British collector. The large metal tube seen on the vehicle contained the rods and cleaning brush for the main gun. The 88mm main gun could be traversed 13 degrees in either direction and could be elevated 14 degrees and depressed 8 degrees. (*David Marian*)

(**Opposite, below**) The Hunting Tank 38 seen here is best known by its unofficial nickname of *Hetzer*. Based on the much-modified chassis of the Panzer 38(t) light tank, the four-man vehicle weighed approximately 32,300lb. It had a length of 20ft 11in, a width of 8ft 7in and a height of 7ft 1in. Top speed on level roads was 26mph with an operational range of 110 miles. (*Patton Museum*)

(**Above**) Taking part in an historical military vehicle event in Great Britain is a restored *Hetzer*. The sloping front glacis is 60mm thick with the sides of the superstructure being only 20mm. The vehicle roof and rear deck were 8mm thick and the hull floor 10mm. The 75mm main gun was limited to a traverse of only 5 degrees to the left and 11 degrees to the right. *(Ian Wilcox)*

(**Opposite, above**) In this picture of a restored *Hetzer* we see the loader's remote-control machine gun on the superstructure roof. Underneath the weapon was the upper portion of the loader's periscope sight. To the right of the machine gun is the gunner's periscope sight and to the left the overhead hatch for the loader. *(Chris Hughes)*

(**Opposite, below**) Seen inside a restored *Hetzer* is the mechanism for aiming and firing the loader's remote-control machine gun on the roof of the vehicle. Unfortunately, the loader had to open the overhead hatch and expose his upper torso to enemy fire to reload the weapon with fifty-round drums. There was authorized stowage on the vehicle for 1,200 machine-gun rounds. *(Chris Hughes)*

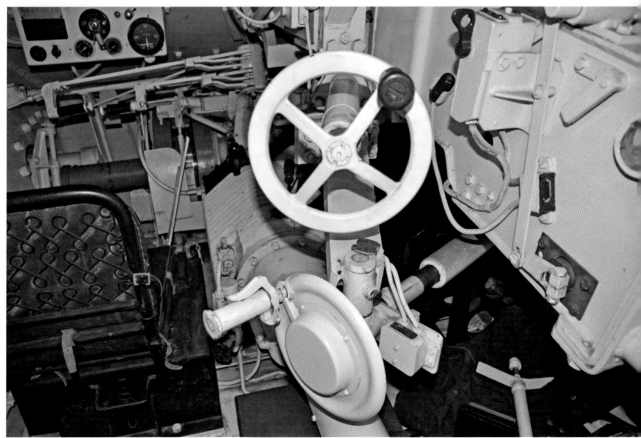

(**Opposite, above**) Belonging to the US army museum system is this preserved *Hetzer*. There was authorized stowage on the vehicle for forty-one rounds of 75mm main gun ammunition. The gun had an internal travel lock that the gunner would release upon the commands of the vehicle commander and relock upon the conclusion of a firing mission. (*Christophe Vallier*)

(**Above**) The *Hetzer* pictured here is shown on display at the now-closed Patton Museum of Armor and Cavalry. The vehicle commander sat directly behind the 75mm main gun on the right side of the vehicle and was provided with an overhead hatch. It was through this overhead hatch that the vehicle commander projected the upper portion of his scissor-type periscope sight. (*Chun-lun Hsu*)

(**Opposite, below**) In this picture taken within a restored *Hetzer* can be seen the gunner's manual traverse and elevation/depression controls for the 75mm main gun. In the lower background in the image are the driver's seat and his controls. To the driver's right is the vehicle transmission. The loader's position was directly behind that of the gunner. As constantly turning the vehicle to aim its main gun strained the original final drive, new stronger ones were fitted on the production line beginning in January 1945. (*Chris Hughes*)

(**Opposite, above**) Belonging to an American collection is this restored *Hetzer*. When originally conceived, it was planned to arm the vehicle with a recoilless rifle. As events unfolded it soon became clear that the recoilless rifle was not going to be available in time. It was decided at the last minute to arm it with the same 75mm main gun as in the StuG III Ausf. G. (*Author's collection*)

(**Opposite, below**) Belonging to the collection of a British museum is this preserved *Hetzer*. It was not originally designed for the mounting of a 75mm main gun but instead a much lighter recoilless rifle. When the gun was installed it led to the overloading of the right-side suspension system and made the vehicle nose-heavy. To compensate for this a number of design fixes were implemented. (*Tank Museum*)

(**Opposite, above**) US army soldiers pass by two knocked-out examples of the *Hetzer*. The driver of the vehicle was typically the last one out in case of an emergency, such as a disabling hit. In August 1944, two handles were welded to the interior roof above the driver's position to assist him in exiting the vehicle as quickly as possible. (*Patton Museum*)

Belonging to the Canadian army museum system is this preserved *Hetzer*. In March 1945 an order went out to the builders of the vehicle to switch from the original gasoline-powered engine to a new more fuel-efficient diesel engine. This order was quickly rescinded as it was clear that it would involve an extensive redesign of the vehicle and a corresponding decrease in the number of *Hetzers* that could be built. *(Paul and Loren Hannah)*

Pictured in a British museum is this early-production Hunting Tiger Sd.Kfz. 186 armed with a 128mm main gun. It was based on the lengthened chassis of the Tiger B heavy tank (also known as the Tiger II). This particular example is one of eleven units built with a Porsche-designed suspension system, which can be identified by there being eight road wheels on either side of the hull. *(Tank Museum)*

Shown here on display at the now-closed US Army Ordnance Museum is a Hunting Tiger Sd.Kfz. 186. It is riding on a Henschel-designed suspension system with nine road wheels on either side of the hull. The vehicle weight is approximately 158,000lb. Length is 25ft 7in with a width of 12ft 3in and a height of 9ft 3in. Top speed on level roads was 24mph with an operational range of 68 miles. *(Christophe Vallier)*

A Hunting Tiger Sd.Kfz. 186 sits abandoned in a German village at the end of the war in Europe. The superstructure frontal armour on the six-man vehicle was 250mm thick with the upper glacis 150mm and the lower front hull 100mm thick. The superstructure sides and rear were 80mm thick, as were the hull side plates.

(Patton Museum)

(**Above**) Many of the surviving examples of the Hunting Tiger Sd.Kfz. 186 were blown up by their crews prior to being abandoned, as is evident in this picture. In many cases the vehicles were not lost to combat action but rather due to mechanical breakdown. Due to a lack of 128mm guns, four units of the Hunting Tiger Sd.Kfz. 186 were armed with the same 88mm main gun that went into the Hunting Panther Sd.Kfz. 173. (*Patton Museum*)

(**Opposite, above**) Pictured is a preserved Italian army Self-Propelled Gun L6/40 that first appeared in service in 1942. It was armed with a 47mm high-velocity anti-tank gun in an open-topped superstructure. The 14,300lb vehicle was crewed by three men. It was 14ft in length, had a width of 6ft 3in and a height of 5ft 6in. It had a top speed on level roads of 26mph and an operational range of 124 miles. (*Christophe Vallier*)

(**Opposite, below**) Being inspected by Allied soldiers is a knocked-out Italian army Self-Propelled Gun 90/53. It is armed with a modified 90mm anti-aircraft gun. The gun shield on the four-man vehicle was 41mm thick. It had a length of 17ft 4in with a width of 7ft 4in and a height of 7ft 5in. The Western Allies first encountered the Self-Propelled Gun 90/53 during the invasion of Sicily in July 1943. (*Patton Museum*)

(**Opposite, above**) Shown here is a nicely-restored example of an Italian army Self-Propelled Gun 90/53 captured in Sicily during the Second World War by the US army. The vehicle was powered by a diesel engine that provided it with a top speed on level roads of 26mph and an operational range of 125 miles. As with so much Italian army equipment, surviving units of the Self-Propelled Gun 90/53 had a second career with the German army following Italy's surrender to the Western Allies in September 1943. (*Paul and Loren Hannah*)

(**Above**) To place as many 90mm gun-armed self-propelled tank destroyers into the field as quickly as possible, Italian industry decided to use existing 4 × 4 and 6 × 6 heavy trucks for the role. Pictured here is a captured example. To steady the vehicle when firing, the trucks were equipped with outriggers, one of which is visible on the rear of the vehicle shown. (*Tank Museum*)

(**Opposite, below**) Seen on display at the former US Army Ordnance Museum is this preserved Japanese army tank destroyer labelled the Type 1 Ho-Ni I. It was based on the chassis of the T97 medium tank and mounted a Type 90 75mm field gun. The US army first encountered the vehicle during the campaign to retake the Philippines between 1944 and 1945 where this particular example was captured. (*Christophe Vallier*)

Chapter Four

Miscellaneous

In the late 1930s, as the German army continued to put into practice its theories of combined-arms warfare centred on the tank, a requirement for an armoured personnel carrier (APC) to accommodate a squad of ten infantrymen appeared. The APC would carry those infantrymen into battle and had to be simple, affordable and built in large numbers. Its main role was to support tanks on the battlefield.

The German army did not have the time to solicit the design and development of a new state-of-the-art APC. It needed something already in the inventory that could be modified for the role. A full-tracked APC was out of the question due to the cost, and the fact that German industry was already struggling to build enough tanks. By default, the German army began looking at the possibility of an armoured half-track.

A Candidate is Selected

The vehicle selected for conversion to an APC had begun its service career with the German army as an unarmoured half-track prime mover and was listed as the Sd.Kfz. 11. Modified to accommodate an armoured body, the machine-gun-armed prototypes appeared in 1938. The first production vehicles began coming off the assembly lines in 1939.

The new APC was originally labelled the *Mittlerer Mannschaftstransportwagen* (Medium Personnel Transport Vehicle) and listed as the Sd.Kfz. 251. In early 1941, the Sd.Kfz. 251 was relabelled the *Mittlerer Schützenpanzerwagen* (Medium Armoured Infantry Vehicle). This reflected the German army's awareness that this was not a simple transport vehicle but a true armoured fighting vehicle.

Although the ordnance number of the Medium Armoured Infantry Vehicle Sd.Kfz. 251 suggests that it came after the Light Armoured Infantry Vehicle Sd.Kfz. 250 discussed in the first chapter of this work, this was not the case. In reality, the Sd.Kfz. 250 series were a smaller sub-variant of the Sd.Kfz. 251 series. Initial production of the Sd.Kfz. 250 series did not begin until June 1941.

Employment

The following extracts appear in an October 1942 American War Department publication. They are translated from a captured manual on a German army Motorized Infantry Regiment equipped with the Sd.Kfz. 251 series:

1. Motorized infantry units form the offensive infantry element in the armoured division. Their strength lies in their speed and cross-country performance, together with the possession of numerous automatic weapons and protective armour.
2. The possession of armoured personnel carriers enables motorized infantry units to overcome comparatively weak opposition without dismounting. They can follow up tank attacks on the field of battle without dismounting.
3. Motorized infantry is characterized by ability to alternate rapidly between fighting from carriers and fighting on foot, and also to combine these two methods of combat.
4. Mobility and the possession of numerous automatic weapons enable motorized infantry units to defend even a broad front against comparatively strong enemy forces.

Base Models

There would be four progressively-improved models of the Sd.Kfz. 251 series: the Ausf. A, B, C and D. Each was a more simplified version of its predecessor in order to cut costs and accelerate production. Lessons learned from combat experience were incorporated into the designs of the Ausf. C and Ausf. D models.

The Ausf. A began coming off the production line in July 1939 and remained in production up until 1941 with 537 units assembled. On the heels of the Ausf. A came the Ausf. B, which was built between 1939 and 1940 resulting in 250 units completed. Production of the Ausf. C began in 1940 alongside the Ausf. B and ended in 1943 with a total of 3,863 units.

The last model of the Sd.Kfz. 251 series built – the Ausf. D – began rolling off the factory floor in September 1943. By the time the war in Europe ended, a total of 11,982 units of the Ausf. D had been fielded.

Rocket-Launcher Kit

For the infantry fire support role, there was a factory-built metal framework kit that fitted over the superstructure of the Sd.Kfz. 251/1 series. Attached to the framework were six 11in or six 15in rockets, with three mounted on either side of the vehicle's superstructure. The individual rockets were shipped in wooden or metal crates that were affixed to the metal framework and doubled as their launcher units. The wooden shipping/launcher crates for the rockets were discarded following firing, whereas the more durable metal shipping/ launcher crates were reused.

Due to the immense back-blast generated by these rockets when fired, the Sd.Kfz. 251 crews typically removed themselves to a safe distance prior to firing. The rockets were not very accurate and were relatively short-ranged. However, when employed as an area fire weapon they could make up for a shortage of conventional artillery pieces.

Sd.Kfz. 251 Variants

A wide range of Sd.Kfz. 251 variants were eventually fielded. Each variant was identified by a forward slash (/) and following number.

Built Upon the A, B and C Models:

Sd.Kfz. 251/1: Armoured personnel carrier.

Sd.Kfz. 251/2: Armed with an 81mm mortar.

Sd.Kfz. 251/3: Radio-equipped command and control vehicle.

Sd.Kfz. 251/4: Prime mover for a 105mm howitzer.

Sd.Kfz. 251/5: Heavy engineering assault vehicle.

Sd.Kfz. 251/6: A version of the Sd.Kfz. 251/3 intended for use by senior officers.

Sd.Kfz. 251/7: A simpler version of the Sd.Kfz. 251/5 considered as a light engineering assault vehicle.

Sd.Kfz. 251/8: Armoured field ambulance.

Sd.Kfz. 251/9: Fire-support version armed with a short-barrel, low-velocity 75mm gun.

Sd.Kfz. 251/10: 37mm anti-tank gun-armed version for platoon leader vehicles.

Sd.Kfz. 251/11: Employed in laying and maintaining telephone and telegraph lines and cables.

Sd.Kfz. 251/12, 13, 14 and 15: Artillery surveying and spotting vehicles of varying configurations.

Sd.Kfz. 251/16: Flame-thrower vehicle.

Sd.Kfz. 251/18: Artillery command post vehicle.

Sd.Kfz. 251/19: Mobile telephone exchange vehicle.

Built Upon the D Model:

Sd.Kfz. 251/1: Armoured personnel carrier.

Sd.Kfz. 251/2: Armed with an 81mm mortar.

Sd.Kfz. 251/3: Radio-equipped command and control vehicle.

Sd.Kfz. 251/4: Prime mover for a long-barrel, high-velocity 75mm anti-tank gun.

Sd.Kfz. 251/9: Fire-support version armed originally with a short-barrel, low-velocity 75mm gun from the early versions of the StuG series vehicles. The second version was armed with a short-barrel, low-velocity howitzer.

Sd.Kfz. 251/10: 37mm anti-tank gun-armed version for platoon leader vehicles.

Sd.Kfz. 251/17: Experimental anti-aircraft vehicle.

Sd.Kfz. 251/19: Mobile telephone exchange vehicle.

Sd.Kfz. 251/20: Infrared-equipped vehicle for illuminating targets for attached tanks.

Sd.Kfz. 251/21: Anti-aircraft vehicle.

Sd.Kfz. 251/22: Armed with a long-barrel, high-velocity 75mm anti-tank gun.

Pre-War Half-Track Anti-Aircraft Vehicles

The German military fielded two self-propelled anti-aircraft vehicles prior to the Second World War. The smaller of the two was armed with a single-barrel, high-velocity 20mm automatic cannon and was based on the chassis of an unarmoured prime mover labelled the Sd.Kfz. 10. With the weapon fitted it was referred to as the 20mm/Self-Propelled Anti-aircraft Gun/on Light Semi-Tracked Vehicle/Sd.Kfz. 10/4. It was fielded by both the German army and German Air Force.

Production of the Sd.Kfz. 10/4 began in 1938 and continued until 1944, with 610 units completed. Early examples lacked armour protection. Combat experience showed this to have been a mistake as the vehicle was often pushed into supporting ground operations. This led the crews of the Sd.Kfz. 10/4 to armour their vehicles themselves with whatever happened to be available. Eventually a factory-installed gun shield and armoured cab appeared.

From a Military Intelligence Service Information Bulletin dated December 1942 comes this translated passage from the captured notes of a commander of a German army anti-aircraft platoon equipped with the Sd.Kfz. 10/4:

> The 20mm gun on a self-propelled mount combines the firepower and mobility of an AA gun with the accuracy and penetration of an AT gun. Its disadvantage is that it is insufficiently armored, and this fault must be offset by good use of ground fire control ... It has been proved that the gun rightly used can put even the heaviest tanks to flight, even if it cannot put them out of action. The most effective range against tanks is under 400 yards. Every effort must be made to attack tanks from the flank.

The 20mm automatic cannon of the Sd.Kfz. 10/4 was designated the 2cm FlaK 30 and first appeared in German army service in 1934 on a two-wheeled towed carriage. In theory, it had a rate of fire of 280 rounds per minute (rpm); in practice that rate of fire was normally restricted to 120 rpm. The maximum horizontal range was approximately 5,000 yards. Vertical range was approximately 12,000ft.

Larger of the Two

The larger of the two pre-war German military self-propelled anti-aircraft vehicles consisted of a single-barrel, high-velocity 37mm automatic gun originally mounted on a towed trailer. It was later fitted onto the chassis of an unarmoured prime mover labelled the Sd.Kfz. 6. With the weapon fitted it was listed as the 37mm Anti-aircraft Gun 36/Self-Propelled Anti-aircraft Gun on Light Semi-Tracked Vehicle/Sd.Kfz. 6/2. Between 1939 and 1943 a total of 339 units were constructed for the German Air Force. Originally unarmoured, the vehicle was eventually fitted with a gun shield.

The 37mm anti-aircraft gun on the Sd.Kfz. 6/2 was designated the 3.7cm FlaK 36. In theory, it had a rate of fire of 250 rpm; in practice this was typically limited to just

120 rpm. The horizontal range for the weapon was approximately 7,160 yards and the vertical range about 16,000ft. The 3.7cm FlaK 36, like the 2cm FlaK 20, was provided with an AP round for employment during ground engagements.

Wartime Half-Track Anti-Aircraft Vehicles

As production of the unarmoured prime mover labelled the Sd.Kfz. 6 was halted in 1943, it was necessary to select a new platform for mounting the 3.7cm FlaK 36. The vehicle chosen was the unarmoured prime mover Sd.Kfz. 7. With the weapon fitted it became the Sd.Kfz. 7/2 of which 123 were built through to October 1944 for the German Air Force. Early-production units lacked armour protection for the crew. This was corrected on later examples, which appeared with a lightly-armoured cab and a weapon gun shield.

The unarmoured prime mover Sd.Kfz. 7 was also chosen to mount a quadruple (four-gun) version of the 2cm FlaK 30 designated the 2cm FlaK 38. With this weapon mounted it became the Sd.Kfz. 7/1 with 319 units constructed by October 1944. With all four guns firing, the 2cm FlaK 38 had a rate of fire in theory of 1,400 rpm; the reality was about 800 rpm. Vertical range of the weapon was 12,300ft with the horizontal range being about 5,300 yards.

There had been plans by the German military to replace the unarmoured prime mover Sd.Kfz. 7. The anticipated replacement would be a simpler, more affordable unarmoured prime mover. Production of the vehicle referred to as the Heavy Semi-Tracked Carrier began in late 1943. Of the 7,484 units ordered, only 825 were ever completed. Beginning in mid-1944, some were provided with an armoured cab and armed with the 3.7cm FlaK 3.

Wartime Full-Tracked Anti-Aircraft Vehicles

As half-tracks lacked the off-road mobility to keep up with tanks and Allied ground-attack aircraft became an ever-increasing threat, in 1943 German industry came up with an evolving series of self-propelled fully-tracked anti-aircraft vehicles. The first was based on the Panzer 38(t) chassis and was labelled the Anti-aircraft Tank 38(t)/Self-Propelled 38(t)/Ausf. L/Sd.Kfz. 140. It was armed with the 2cm FlaK 30 in an open-topped armoured superstructure. A total of 140 units were built between November 1943 and February 1944 for the German army.

The Sd.Kfz. 140 was seen only as an interim vehicle until a series of evolving anti-aircraft tanks based on the chassis of the Panzer IV medium tank could be fielded in sufficient numbers. The first was the 37mm/Self-Propelled Anti-aircraft Gun on Tank Chassis/Sd.Kfz. 161/3. Rather than the single-barrel 3.7cm FlaK 36, it was armed with an improved single-barrel version designated the 3.7cm FlaK 43.

When not in action the weapon and the gun crew of the Sd.Kfz. 161/3 were protected by a four-sided, vertical, open-topped armoured enclosure. Due to its box-like silhouette with the armour enclosure folded up, it was nicknamed the *Möbelwagen* (Furniture Van). To engage the enemy, the four sides of the armoured enclosure were lowered to the horizontal. This provided the onboard 37mm automatic gun with 360 degrees of traverse. A total of 240 units of the Sd.Kfz. 161/3 were provided to the German army between March 1944 and March 1945.

Next in line was the Anti-aircraft Tank IV/20mm/Quadruple Sd.Kfz. 161/4. It was nicknamed the *Wirbelwind* (Whirlwind). It was armed with the four-gun 2cm FlaK 38, with the weapon and gun crew protected by an open-topped, multi-angled turret of armour that was 16mm thick. Due to the shape of the turret, it was also nicknamed the *Keksdose* (Biscuit Tin). A total of eighty-six units of the Whirlwind/Biscuit Tin were constructed between July and November 1944 for the German army.

As the 20mm projectiles of the 2cm FlaK 38 lacked the necessary range and knock-down power to deal with more heavily-armed, late-war Allied ground-attack aircraft, industry came up with another version armed with a single-barrel 3.7cm FlaK 36 in an open-topped turret similar to the Whirlwind. It was labelled the Anti-aircraft Tank IV/3.7cm Anti-aircraft Gun and nicknamed the *Ostwind* (East Wind). Forty-three units of the vehicle were delivered between December 1944 and March 1945.

The planned replacement for the Whirlwind and the East Wind was another Panzer IV-based anti-aircraft tank labelled the Light Anti-aircraft Tank IV/30mm Gun. It was nicknamed the *Kugelblitz* (Ball Lightning) and was armed with two 30mm anti-aircraft guns designated the MK103/38. They were mounted in a fully-armoured turret sphere that traversed and elevated in a low-slung, open-topped turret. Only two were completed before the war in Europe ended and these never saw action.

Full-Tracked Command and Control Vehicles

The German army was an early convert to the idea that the radio was an important force multiplier for its armoured forces. This resulted in the production between 1935 and 1937 of 190 units of a specialized radio-equipped command and control vehicle. It was based on the chassis of the Panzer I light tank with a raised super-structure and no turret. It was labelled the Small Command Tank/Sd.Kfz. 265.

Next in line was a command and control vehicle based on the Panzer III medium tank. Referred to as 'Large Command Tanks', the first three versions listed as Sd.Kfz. 266, 267 and 268 were armed only with machine guns. This fact was hidden from any opponents by fitting them with dummy main gun barrels. A total of 220 units of the first three command and control models of the Panzer III were built between June 1938 and June 1942.

Change is Mandated

In January 1943, the German army decided that there would be no more specially-designed command and control tanks built. All future examples would be based on converting existing gun-armed tanks for the role. A total of 235 units of the Panzer III Ausf. H, J and M were therefore converted to the command and control role between August 1943 and February 1944. They retained the standard gun-armed version inventory number of Sd.Kfz. 141.

As the Panzer III medium tank series was being phased out of front-line service by 1943 and replaced by the Panzer IV medium tank series, the need for a command and control version of the latter appeared. This requirement was satisfied by the construction of ninety-seven units of such a vehicle in 1944. They retained the standard gun-armed version inventory number of Sd.Kfz. 161.

As the Panzer IV was in turn being replaced by the Panther tank series, a corresponding command and control version appeared. A total of 329 units of the Panther tank series were converted into command and control vehicles between May 1943 and February 1945. These retained the standard gun-armed version inventory number of Sd.Kfz. 171.

An unknown number of Tiger B tanks were also converted to the command and control version. Depending on the radio configuration they were listed as either the Sd.Kfz. 267 or Sd.Kfz. 268. The standard model of the tank was listed as the Sd.Kfz. 182, of which 489 were produced between January 1944 and March 1945.

Full-Tracked Artillery Forward Observers' Vehicles

There was a specialized model of the Panzer III for employment by artillery forward observers. The vehicle was based on the Ausf. E and H models and was armed only with a machine gun. To disguise its role on the battlefield it was fitted with a dummy main gun barrel. A total of 262 vehicles were converted between February 1943 and April 1944.

There were also ninety units of the Panzer IV converted into an artillery forward observer's vehicle between July 1944 and March 1945. Unlike the Panzer III-based version, it retained its main armament. A total of forty-one units of the Panther were converted for the artillery observer role. Like the Panzer III artillery observation vehicle, the Panther-based version was armed only with machine guns and featured a dummy main gun barrel to hide that fact.

Self-Propelled Artillery

In the years before the Second World War, the Germany army had not identified a requirement for self-propelled artillery. It was envisioned that the German Air Force's ground-attack aircraft would provide the necessary firepower to support its fast-moving armoured columns during the short campaigns anticipated. Once the German army realized that this was not going to be a short war, industry responded with a variety of self-propelled artillery pieces for the army's armoured forces.

150mm Self-Propelled Howitzers

The first self-propelled artillery piece for the German army consisted of the chassis of the obsolete Panzer I light tank upon which a 150mm howitzer was mounted in a tall open-topped superstructure. Its official designation was 150mm Self-Propelled/ Tank I Ausf. B. Thirty-eight units were constructed in early 1940, with some lasting in service until 1943. The original towed version of the 150mm howitzer had entered into German army service in 1933 as the sIG (*schweres Infanterie Geschütz*) 33 and was classified as an infantry heavy field cannon.

As the chassis of the Panzer I light tank proved too small for the effective operation of the 150mm howitzer and the height of the vehicle a disadvantage on the battlefield, industry decided to employ a lengthened open-topped chassis of the Panzer II light tank as the platform for the mounting of the 150mm howitzer. Only twelve units were built in late 1941 and all were sent to North Africa to serve with the famed German army Afrika Korps. None would survive combat in that theatre of operations.

Foreign-Based 155mm Self-Propelled Howitzers

Next in line for the mounting of the 150mm howitzer was the modified chassis of the Panzer 38(t) light tank. The resulting vehicle was officially nicknamed the *Grille* (Cricket), of which ninety units were constructed between February and April 1943. Like its two predecessors, the 150mm howitzer was mounted on the forward portion of the chassis as the vehicle's engine remained in the rear hull. It was listed as the Sd.Kfz. 138/1.

The follow-on version of the four-man Cricket had the location of the engine and 150mm howitzer reversed. This design layout was considered much more satisfactory than the original for the servicing of the weapon. A total of 282 units of this version of the Cricket were constructed between April 1943 and September 1944. It retained the Sd.Kfz. 138/1 listing.

In November 1944, it was decided to mount the 150mm howitzer on the modified chassis of the *Hetzer* tank destroyer, which itself was based on the chassis of the Panzer 38(t) light tank. Instead of mounting the weapon in the rear of the vehicle as had been done with the second model of the Cricket, the rear engine arrangement of the *Hetzer* was retained and the weapon mounted at the front of the chassis and protected by an open-topped superstructure. Only thirty units of this vehicle were built in December 1944.

As an expedient measure, ninety-four units of a captured French army armoured logistical support vehicle referred to as the Lorraine 37L were modified in 1942 to mount the standard German army 150mm howitzer. Labelled as a 155mm Self-Propelled Field Howitzer on Captured Tracked Carrier Chassis, it was listed as the Sd. 135/1. Forty units of the vehicle saw service in the North Africa theatre of

> ## German Self-Propelled Artillery Employment
>
> In the US War Department Handbook on German Military Forces, published in March 1945, appear these passages describing the tactical employment of German self-propelled artillery in the attack:
>
> Artillery support is of decisive importance for the preparation and the successful conduct of a tank attack. A unified command for the entire artillery controls the artillery fire as long as the infantry and tank units are fighting on the same line. When the tanks break through enemy forward defense lines, the self-propelled artillery or any other artillery battalion designated for the support of the tank unit is placed under the command of the tank unit commander.
>
> The mission of the artillery preparation before the attack is to destroy, or at least to neutralize the opponent's antitank defense in the area between the line of contact and the regimental reserve line. Continuous counterbattery fire prevents the enemy from shelling the tank assembly area and from breaking up the preparation of the tank attack.
>
> Liaison between artillery and tanks during the attack is established by the commanding officers and the artillery liaison group, which normally moves with the first wave. Artillery forward observers, if possible in armored observation posts [vehicles] ride with the most forward elements. A German field expedient is for the tank unit to take along a forward observer in one of its tanks. It often happens that the tankman himself has to take over the observation for the artillery.

operations with the German army. Fifty-four units of the vehicle were still marked in service in France in early 1944.

The Japanese army also fielded a small number of self-propelled 150mm artillery pieces based on Type 97 medium tank chassis. It was referred to as the Type 38 HO-RO and began entering service in 1942. The weapon and gun crew were protected by an open-topped superstructure of riveted construction.

The Larger 150mm Howitzer

Besides the 150mm sIG 33 Infantry Heavy Field Cannon mounted on a variety of self-propelled platforms, the German army fielded in 1939 the 150mm Heavy Field Howitzer listed as the sFH (*schwere Feldhaubitze*) 18/1 L/30 with a barrel length of 21ft. By way of comparison the 150mm sIG 33 Infantry Heavy Field Cannon had a barrel length of just 5ft 5in.

The chassis eventually chosen for mounting the 150mm Heavy Field Howitzer sFH 18/1 L/30 was the same employed by the Hornet/Rhinoceros. With the weapon mounted on the vehicle it was officially nicknamed the *Hummel* (Bumblebee) and listed as the Sd.Kfz. 165. A total of 714 units were built between early 1943 and 1945.

Because the vehicle only had authorized stowage for 18 rounds, 157 units of a weaponless version of the *Hummel* were employed as ammunition resupply vehicles.

105mm Self-Propelled Howitzers

Beginning in 1941, industry had proposed to the German army the mounting of its standard 105mm howitzer on the chassis of a vehicle based on components of the Panzer IV medium tank. Eight experimental units were constructed in 1942 with the weapon fitted in a semi-traversable open-topped turret. This was followed by several experimental units in 1943, based upon a chassis that combined components of the Panzer III and Panzer IV medium tanks.

The German army preferred to see the 105mm light field howitzer (designated the LEFH 18M) mounted on the modified chassis of the Panzer II light tank. This led to the building of the Sd.Kfz. 124, officially nicknamed the *Wespe* (Wasp). Production of the Wasp began in February 1943 and ended in July 1944 with 676 units constructed. In addition, 159 units of an ammunition resupply vehicle based on the same chassis were built to serve alongside it on the battlefield.

Foreign-Based 105mm Self-Propelled Howitzers

In 1942 plans had called for the conversion of sixty units of a captured French army armoured logistical support vehicle, referred to as the Lorraine 37L, to mount the standard German army 105mm howitzer; however, in the end only twelve were constructed. The weapon was mounted at the rear of the chassis and protected by an open-topped superstructure.

The chassis of a French army light tank labelled the Hotchkiss H39 was also converted by the Germans for use as a platform for the 105mm howitzer. Referred to as the 105mm Light Field Howitzer on Captured Light Tank Chassis 39H(f), a total of forty-eight units were constructed in 1942.

Another captured French army light tank designated the FCM 36 was also converted to mount a 105mm howitzer. Only twelve units were constructed in 1942. In the same year, the Germans employed the chassis of sixteen units of the French army heavy tank Char-1 bis as a platform for the German 105mm howitzer. It was designated the 105mm Light Field Howitzer on Captured Heavy Tank Chassis B-2(f).

Rocket-Firing Vehicles

Because conventional wheeled trucks proved unsuitable for use on the Eastern Front due to the lack of paved roads, it was decided in 1942 to improve the off-road performance of the standard German army 3-ton-capacity 4 x 4 wheeled trucks by replacing their rear wheels with a half-track-type suspension system. This was applied across the board to three different builders' products. The resulting vehicles were referred to as the *Maultier* (Mule).

In 1943, the firm Opel was contracted to build an armoured version of the Mule for mounting a ten-round 8in rocket-launcher labelled the *Nebelwerfer* (Smoke Mortar) 42 on the roof of its rear superstructure. The resulting vehicle was listed as the Sd.Kfz. 4/1. Some were fitted with a twenty-four-rail launcher unit named the 8cm *R-Vielfachwerfer* (3in multiple rocket-launcher). In total, 300 units were constructed with another 289 unarmed units being assigned as ammunition resupply vehicles. The latter were listed as the Sd.Kfz. 4.

Flame-Thrower Tanks

A total of 155 units of a vehicle labelled the Panzer II Flame-thrower Ausf. A and Ausf. B and listed as the Sd.Kfz. 122 were built between January and March 1942. It had a one-man turret armed with a machine gun. On either side of the front superstructure were the flame guns. Combat experience in the Soviet Union in 1941 showed them to be highly vulnerable to enemy fire. All surviving units were returned to Germany for conversion into tank destroyers in early 1942.

The replacement for the Panzer II flame-thrower tank was based on the chassis of the Panzer III Ausf. M. In place of its standard 50mm main gun it was fitted with a turret-mounted flame gun. To disguise the vehicle's role on the battlefield it had a dummy main gun barrel through which the flaming gasoline was expelled. A total of 100 were built between February and April 1943. It was listed as the Sd.Kfz. 141/3.

The last flame-thrower tanks placed into service by the German army were twenty units converted from the *Hetzer* in December 1944. Labelled the Flame-Thrower Tank 38(t), they were intended for use during the German offensive into Belgium in the winter of 1944. That campaign was named Operation WATCH ON THE RHINE by the German military and the Ardennes Counter-offensive by the Western Allies. Like the Panzer III-based flame-thrower tank, the *Hetzer* version was fitted with a dummy main gun barrel.

Prior to the Second World War the Italian army had identified a requirement for a flame-thrower tank. In 1933 there appeared a two-man vehicle referred to as the L3-33 *Lancia Fiamme* (flame-thrower). It was based on the machine-gun-armed Carro Veloce (Fast Tank) CV-35 tankette. The fuel for the front superstructure-mounted flame gun was either towed behind the vehicle in a two-wheeled trailer or in a large steel tank mounted on top of the engine compartment. The number built is unknown.

Urban Assault Vehicles

For dealing with heavily-fortified defensive positions in urban areas, industry provided the German army with several specialized urban assault-type vehicles. Each mounted a progressively larger weapon intended only for direct fire. Reflecting their need for dealing with enemy fire from all directions, the urban assault vehicles were well-armoured including roof armour.

The first was the Assault Infantry Gu 33B based on the chassis of the Panzer III medium tank. Only twenty-four units were assembled between December 1941 and October 1942. It was armed with the same 150mm sIG 33 Infantry Heavy Field Cannon that had been mounted on the modified chassis of the Panzer I, Panzer II, Panzer 38(t) and captured French army light tanks converted into self-propelled artillery pieces.

The second was referred to as the 'Assault Panzer IV' or 'Assault Panzer 43'. It was based on the chassis of the Panzer IV medium tank. A total of 308 units were completed between April 1943 and March 1945. It was armed with a Czech-designed and built 150mm howitzer designated the StuH43 L/12. It fired the same rounds as the 150mm sIG 33 Infantry Heavy Field Cannon. Many sources suggest that the vehicle's unofficial nickname was *Brummbär* (Grumbling Bear or 'Grouch').

Between August and December 1944 industry converted eighteen units of the Tiger E heavy tank into what was known as the 380mm RW61 Assault-Mortar Tiger. The rounds fired by the vehicle were rocket-assisted with the exhaust gases vented through small holes in the muzzle end of the weapon's barrel. The weapon itself was based on a depth-charge-launcher developed for the German navy. The rounds – either HE or HEAT – were 5ft long and weighed up to 772lb. The HEAT round could penetrate up to 8ft of reinforced concrete.

Odds and Ends

Among the vast haul of military equipment acquired by the German army from the French army in 1941 were approximately 6,000 units of the fully-tracked Renault UE. It was a small two-man armoured but unarmed logistical supply vehicle that had begun entering French army service in 1931. Some of those taken into service by the German army were armed with a variety of weapons ranging from machine guns to small anti-tank guns.

Brought into German army service in 1941 were an unknown number of pre-war French army unarmoured half-tracks labelled the *Somua* MCG. The French army employed them as cargo-hauling vehicles or prime movers. The German army had a number of them fitted with armoured bodies and used them as everything from armoured personnel carriers to weapon carriers. Armament fitted included everything from machine guns to rockets and mortars.

Another French army vehicle brought into German army service was a full-tracked armoured reconnaissance light tank labelled the AMR35. The German army had the vehicle's original machine-gun-armed turret and superstructure removed. In their place appeared an open-topped three-sided superstructure that protected an 80mm mortar and crew. The number converted is unknown. It was labelled the 81mm Heavy Mortar 34 Armoured Scout Car AMR35(f).

Among the booty captured from the British army during the German military invasion of France were an unknown number of the full-tracked Universal Carriers. The small armoured vehicle was employed by the German army as a platform for a variety of weapons ranging from machine guns to small anti-tank guns as well as anti-aircraft guns.

(**Below**) When the German army decided that it needed infantry to accompany its tanks into battle, a requirement arose for a suitable armoured transport vehicle that could be fielded rapidly. A full-tracked model was rejected as industry was already having problems with building sufficient tanks. This led to the decision to modify the existing Sd.Kfz. 11 half-track prime mover seen here with an armoured body. (*Christophe Vallier*)

(**Opposite, above**) Sporting an armoured body, the unarmoured prime mover Sd.Kfz. 11 became the Sd.Kfz. 251. The version pictured was the original model labelled the Ausf. A. Spotting features not seen on subsequent versions are the lack of an armoured shield for the machine gun mounted at the front of the superstructure and the two armoured visors on either side of the rear troop compartment. (*Patton Museum*)

(**Opposite, below**) A design feature of the first three models of the Sd.Kfz. 251 was the rear, outward-extending troop compartments. The rear doors on the vehicles were built up from two pieces of armour bolted together and were mounted on hinged swing-out arms. With the two follow-on models of the Sd.Kfz. 251, the two panels that made up the rear troop compartment doors were welded together. (*Patton Museum*)

(**Above**) A spotting feature of the Sd.Kfz. 251 Ausf. B was the addition of a gun shield for the front superstructure-mounted machine gun. The Ausf. B retained the two-piece nose plates of the Ausf. A model. The closed armoured flap in the lower nose plate is the air intake for the radiator and those on either side of the engine compartment were intended to help cool the engine. (*Patton Museum*)

(**Opposite, above**) The replacement for the first two models of the Sd.Kfz. 251 was the Ausf. C version seen here. Spotting features of this model were the one-piece flat nose plate and the armoured vent covers that replaced the original armoured engine cooling flaps. As some manufacturers of the Sd.Kfz. 251 Ausf. C lacked the ability to weld armour plate, they were allowed to build them with riveting as is evident in this photograph. (*Tank Museum*)

(**Opposite, below**) To speed up production of the Sd.Kfz. 251 series the vehicle's design was greatly simplified by reducing the number of armour plates employed in its construction by nearly half. This resulted in the fielding of the final model of the Sd.Kfz. 251 series, the Ausf. D seen here. It had a length of 19ft 7in, a width of 6ft 11in and a height of 5ft 9in. (*Ian Wilcox*)

(**Opposite, above**) A key identifying feature of the Sd.Kfz. 251 Ausf. D was the sharply-angled rear troop compartment of the vehicle seen here. Visible are the two large hinged doors that replaced the more complex design of the two doors on earlier versions. At the top of the rear superstructure is the mount for a second machine gun not fitted on this example. (*Patton Museum*)

(**Opposite, below**) Belonging to the now-closed Military Vehicle Technology Foundation is this restored Sd.Kfz. 251 Ausf. D. The flat one-piece nose plate on the vehicle was 15mm thick. On the front of the vehicle's superstructure the armour was 10mm thick and along the sides 8mm. The engine cooling vents were located under the engine compartment side armour. (*Chris Hughes*)

(**Opposite, above**) Pictured are the two hatches that provided access to the liquid-cooled, gasoline-powered engine of a restored Sd.Kfz. 251 Ausf. D. This was the same arrangement on the three previous models in the Sd.Kfz. 251 series. The six-cylinder engine provided the vehicle with a top speed on level roads of 33mph and an operational range of 186 miles. (*Charles Kliment*)

(**Opposite, above**) Taking part in an historical military vehicle event in Great Britain is this restored Sd.Kfz. 251 Ausf. D. The vehicle weighed approximately 18,000lb, with the previous versions weighing just a bit less. Note that the separate stowage boxes that had been part of the three earlier models were incorporated into the vehicle's superstructure in lieu of the mudguards of earlier versions. (*Ian Wilcox*)

(**Opposite, below**) On display in a French museum is this restored Sd.Kfz. 251/7 Ausf. D. It was considered a light assault *Pioneer* (Engineering) vehicle with two versions built, differing only in stowage arrangements. Both had two metal support brackets on either side of the vehicle's upper superstructure to carry small portable bridges as can be seen in this photograph. (*Christophe Vallier*)

(**Above**) A restored Sd.Kfz. 251 Ausf. D is pictured here. The front wheels on the entire Sd.Kfz. 251 series were neither powered nor had brakes. They only supported the weight of the vehicle's engine and nose plate/plates and provided steering. During slight turns the vehicle's steering only turned the front wheels. Once the turn became wider than 15 degrees, the vehicle's tank-type clutch and brake steering mechanism took over. (*Pierre-Olivier Buan*)

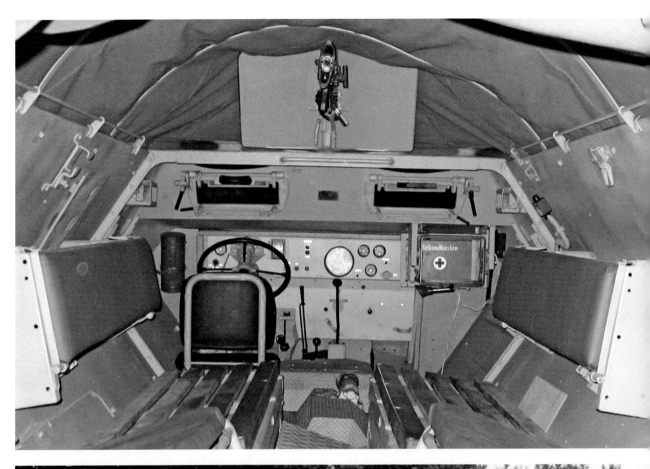

(**Opposite, above**) The interior of a restored Sd.Kfz. 251/7 Ausf. D. Note the canvas foul weather tarp has been erected, which is supported by removable metal hoops. As with everything else on the Ausf. D, the interior accommodations were simplified. Instead of the padded leather bench seats of earlier models of the Sd.Kfz. 251, in the Ausf. D they were replaced by simple wooden slat benches as pictured here. (*Frank Schulz*)

(**Opposite, below**) Belonging to the collection of a German museum is this restored Sd.Kfz. 251/7 Ausf. D light assault *Pionier* (Engineering) vehicle. The small portable bridge sections often carried on these vehicles are not fitted. However, the space between them has been built into an additional stowage compartment. The vehicle is towing a 75mm anti-tank gun. (*Thomas Anderson*)

(**Above**) Beginning with the earliest model of the Sd.Kfz. 251 series – the Ausf. A – there appeared a version designated the Sd.Kfz. 251/10 that was armed with the standard 37mm anti-tank gun as seen here. The vehicle had a crew of five with authorized stowage for 168 main gun rounds. It was also armed with a machine gun. (*Patton Museum*)

(**Opposite, above**) Pictured is an Sd.Kfz. 251/9 armed with a 75mm gun and based on the Ausf. C model. An official nickname for the short-barrel weapon was *Stummel* (Stump). On these early-production units the 75mm gun was located on the front right-hand side of the superstructure as seen in this photograph. The vehicle had a crew of three. *(Patton Museum)*

(**Opposite, below**) In this picture of a preserved Sd.Kfz. 251/9 we can see the breech of the 75mm gun as well as the gunner's seat and his sighting system. The driver's position is in front of and below the gunner's seat. The third member of the vehicle's crew would be the loader. A spent cartridge case ejected from the weapon's breech would strike the rear of the recoil guard and drop to the vehicle's floor. *(Frank Schulz)*

(**Above**) Belonging to the US army museum system is this preserved Sd.Kfz. 251/9 based on the Ausf. D model. The new gun shield for the vehicle's weapon first appeared on new-production units of the Sd.Kfz. 251/9 in 1944. The vehicle had authorized stowage for fifty-four main gun rounds and was armed with two machine guns. *(Rob Cogan)*

In December 1944, Hitler ordered that as many long-barrel, high-velocity anti-tank guns as possible be mounted on whatever self-propelled platforms could support them. This resulted in the Sd.Kfz. 251/22 based on the Ausf. D chassis seen here. It was this same decree that resulted in the production of the Heavy Armoured Car (75mm Anti-tank Gun 40) Sd.Kfz. 234/4. *(National Archives)*

Visible in this photograph is one of the two flame guns fitted to the rear superstructure of an Sd.Kfz. 251/16. This version appeared in service beginning in January 1943. The stowage tanks on board the vehicle held 185 gallons of fuel. This allowed for approximately eighty two-second bursts of flame. Depending on wind conditions, the flame guns had a range of up to 38 yards. *(Patton Museum)*

Specially designed for a German Air Force requirement was the Sd.Kfz. 251/17 seen here. It was based on the chassis of the Ausf. C and armed with a single-barrel 20mm automatic cannon designated the 2cm FlaK 38. There was authorized stowage for 600 rounds of 20mm ammunition on board the vehicle. Only ten units were built before it was decided that the vehicle would be too costly to build in large numbers. (*Patton Museum*)

The German army borrowed and modified for its own use an anti-aircraft pedestal mount originally developed for the German navy armed with three automatic cannons. The original trial units were fitted to the Sd.Kfz. 251 Ausf. C model as seen here. The production model that began appearing in August 1944 was based on the Ausf. D model and listed as the Sd.Kfz. 251/21. (*Patton Museum*)

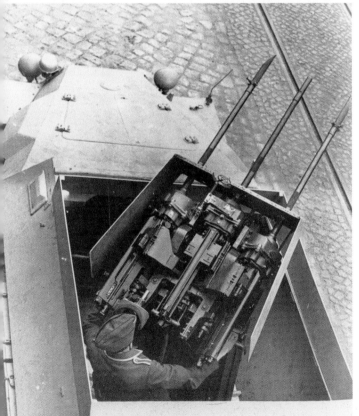

(**Opposite, above**) An add-on kit for the Sd.Kfz. 251/1 consisted of a metal frame that fitted over the vehicle's superstructure. Fastened to the lower portion of the frame on both sides of the vehicle were attachment points for either metal or wooden frame crates as seen here. Each crate contained either an 11in or 15in rocket, which was launched from its stowage crate. (*Patton Museum*)

(**Opposite, below**) Pictured here is a captured Sd.Kfz. 10/4 armed with a shield-protected 20mm automatic cannon labelled the 2cm FlaK 30. This was the German military's first self-propelled anti-aircraft vehicle employed by both their army and air force. When originally fielded, the weapon lacked a gun shield. Ammunition was stored on board the Sd.Kfz. 10/4 and in a small two-wheeled trailer normally towed behind the vehicle. (*Patton Museum*)

(**Above**) Following the invasion of the Soviet Union in 1941, the crews of the Sd.Kfz. 10/4 often found themselves pressed into the ground support role. This resulted in many of them being fitted with improvised armour protection as seen in this photograph. As time went on, new-production units of the Sd.Kfz. 10/4 were fitted with an armoured cab. (*Patton Museum*)

Among the many French army vehicles acquired by the German army in 1940 were almost 2,000 units of an unarmoured half-track labelled the P107. Beginning in 1944, it was decided to armour an unknown number for use in a variety of roles. The example pictured here was configured as an anti-aircraft vehicle and armed with a single-barrel 2cm (20mm) FlaK 30 gun. The official German designation was U-304(f). *(Christophe Vallier)*

Barely visible in this wartime picture is a camouflaged *Flakpanzer* (anti-aircraft tank) 38(t) armed with a single-barrel 2cm (20mm) FlaK 30 gun. The first of 141 units of the vehicle off the assembly lines were issued to units in the field in early 1944. The weapon had 360 degrees traverse with 360 rounds carried on board. *(Patton Museum)*

Another German military self-propelled anti-aircraft vehicle that first entered service prior to the Second World War was the Sd.Kfz. 6/2 pictured here. It was armed with the 3.7cm (37mm) FlaK 36 L/98 gun, which upon lowering the side panels of the rear cargo bay had 360 degrees of traverse. Ammunition for the vehicle was carried in a two-wheeled trailer towed behind the vehicle. (*Patton Museum*)

Pictured here is an armoured half-track vehicle labelled the *Schwerer Wehrmachtschlepper Gepanzerte Ausführung*. Translated it becomes the Heavy Wehrmacht Tractor/ Armoured Model. This example is armed with a 3.7cm (37mm) FlaK 36 L/98 gun and began service in 1944. The armoured cab had a maximum armour thickness of 15mm. (*Patton Museum*)

(**Opposite, above**) On display in a German museum is this restored Sd.Kfz. 7/1 armed with a four-barrel 2cm (20mm) FV38 gun mount. Early-production units lacked the armoured cab. Armour on the driver's cab was 8mm thick. The same vehicle with and without an armoured cab was alternatively armed with a 3.7cm (37mm) FlaK 36 L/98 gun and designated the Sd.Kfz. 7/2. *(Frank Schulz)*

(**Above**) Shown here is a 3.7cm *Flak auf Fahrgestell Panzerkampfwagen* IV (Sf) Sd.Kfz. 161/3. Translated it is the 37mm Anti-aircraft Gun/Tank Chassis IV/Self-Propelled Sd.Kfz. 161/3. The vehicle was an expedient to provide the 3.7cm (37mm) FlaK 36 L/98 gun with the same off-road mobility as the tanks it was supposed to protect as half-tracks lacked the off-road ability of full-tracked vehicles. *(Patton Museum)*

(**Opposite, below**) Belonging to the collection of a French museum is this 37mm Anti-aircraft Gun/Tank Chassis IV/ Self-Propelled Sd.Kfz. 161/3. With this particular vehicle the four-sided superstructure, which was lowered when firing the weapon, is in the raised position to provide maximum protection for the gun crew. The slab-sided appearance resulted in it being nicknamed the *Möbelwagen* (Furniture Van). *(Christophe Vallier)*

(**Opposite, above**) Pictured here is a preserved *Flakpanzer* IV/2cm named the *Wirbelwind* on display at a Canadian museum. Translated it is the Anti-aircraft Tank IV/Quadruple 20mm Gun/Whirlwind. The Panzer IV chassis employed to mount the newly-designed armoured turret were not new-built vehicles but those returned from the various combat theatres for overhaul. *(Paul and Loren Hannah)*

(**Above**) Following the *Flakpanzer* IV/2cm *Vierling* off the assembly line was another anti-aircraft tank based on the chassis of rebuilt Panzer IVs and named the *Ostwind* (East Wind). This one was armed with a single-barrel 3.7cm (37mm) FlaK 36 L/98 gun in a multi-angled turret similar to the one designed for its predecessor. The turret housing the 37mm automatic cannon was 25mm thick all round. *(Patton Museum)*

(**Opposite, below**) The planned replacement for the *Möbelwagen* and the *Ostwind* was to be the anti-aircraft vehicle pictured here. It was referred to as the *Liechte Flakpanzer* IV/3cm and officially nicknamed the *Kugelblitz* (Ball Lightning). It was to be armed with two 30mm automatic cannons in a fully-enclosed mount. The war ended with only two units completed. *(Patton Museum)*

In the collection of a British museum is this machine-gun-armed *Kleiner Panzerbefehlswagen* Sd.Kfz. 265 that translated as Light Armoured Command Tank Sd.Kfz. 265. The vehicle first appeared in German army service in 1935. Early-production units had only a split overhead hatch in the roof of the superstructure. Later-production units as pictured were fitted with a vehicle commander's cupola as seen here. *(Tank Museum)*

Combat experience soon taught the German army that specialized tank-based command vehicles were subject to early destruction. The answer to this issue was to modify at the factory a certain number of the standard gun-armed tanks with additional radios. Pictured here is a restored Panther Ausf. A Sd. Kfz. 171. The only identifying features of the command tanks like the one pictured are additional radio antennas. *(Thomas Anderson)*

The first self-propelled artillery piece in the German army was the vehicle seen here. It consisted of the chassis of a Panzer I light tank upon which a large 150mm howitzer was mounted. The weapon and gun crew were protected by the tall three-sided open-topped superstructure visible in the photograph. The superstructure was 13mm thick and gave the vehicle a height of 9ft 2in. *(Tank Museum)*

The crudely-made and tall superstructure of the 150mm howitzer mounted on the Panzer I light tank chassis was not a successful match. This led to the mounting of the 150mm howitzer on the chassis of à modified Panzer II light tank chassis as seen here. The four-man vehicle had onboard stowage for thirty rounds. The vehicle height was 6ft 3in. *(Tank Museum)*

(**Opposite, above**) Neither the Panzer I nor Panzer II light tank chassis proved optimum for the mounting of a 150mm howitzer. This led to the weapon being mounted on a modified version of the chassis of the Panzer 38(t) light tank as pictured here. The resulting vehicle was officially nicknamed the *Grille* (Cricket) and listed as the Sd.Kfz. 138/1. (*Patton Museum*)

(**Above**) The mounting of the 150mm howitzer of the *Grille* at the front of the chassis and retaining the engine in the rear hull was not the most effective arrangement. This led to a second version of the vehicle seen here with the weapon and engine reversed. This restored example belongs to an American museum. (*Paul and Loren Hannah*)

(**Opposite, below**) By August 1944, industry was running out of the chassis of the Panzer 38(t) light tank to convert into the 150mm howitzer-armed *Grille*. As the demand for the vehicle had not waned, it was decided to use components from the *Hetzer* chassis for mounting the 150mm howitzer. The resulting vehicle is seen here. Less than thirty units were completed before the war ended. (*Charles Kliment*)

(**Above**) Another vehicle pressed into service by the German army as a platform for the 150mm howitzer was a captured French army armoured prime mover labelled the 37L. When fitted with the weapon in an open-topped superstructure it became the 15cm Sfh13/1 (Sf) *auf Geschützwagen Lorraine Schlepper* (f) Sd.Kfz. 135/1. There was also a version of the vehicle armed with a 105mm howitzer. (*Tank Museum*)

(**Opposite, above**) A successful mating of the chassis of the Panzer II light tank and 105mm howitzer is shown here in a French museum. It was officially nicknamed the *Wespe* (Wasp) and listed as the Sd.Kfz. 124. The five-man vehicle weighed approximately 25,000lb. It was 15ft 8in in length with a width of 7ft 5in and a height of 7ft 5in. (*Christophe Vallier*)

(**Opposite, below**) Captured French army light tanks were also employed to mount the German army 105mm howitzer. The combination seen here at a French museum was designated the 10.5cm leFH18 (Sf) *auf Geschütz-wagen* 39H(f). The open-topped superstructure on the vehicle was 20mm on the front and sides and 10mm on the rear. (*Christophe Vallier*)

(**Opposite, above**) In 1942, industry was starting the development of a self-propelled 105mm howitzer mounted in a 360-degree traversable turret. It was to be designated the *Geschützwagen* (Gun Carriage) III/IV. An interesting feature was that an onboard crane could dismount the 105mm howitzer-armed turret if required. Pictured here is the single preserved example of three prototypes completed. (*Paul and Loren Hannah*)

(**Opposite, below**) Belonging to the collection of a German museum is this restored example of a self-propelled artillery piece officially nicknamed the *Hummel* (Bumblebee). It was armed with a long-barrel 150mm howitzer designated the 15cm Sfh18/1 L/30. It was based on the chassis of the *Geschützwagen* III/IV. (*Andreas Kirchhoff*)

(**Above**) In the collection of a French museum is this preserved *Hummel*, which was listed as the Sd.Kfz. 165. The vehicle had a six-man crew and weighed approximately 54,000lb. It was 23ft 5in in length with a width of 9ft 7in and a height of 9ft 2in. There was authorized stowage on board for eighteen main gun rounds. (*Christophe Vallier*)

(**Opposite, above**) The German army contracted for the construction of an armoured half-track fitted with a ten-barrel 150mm rocket-launcher system as pictured here. The armoured half-track was based on an unarmoured half-track prime mover referred to as the *Maultier* (Mule). Its official designation was the 15cm *Panzerwerfer* 42 (Sf) Sd.Kfz. 4/1. The three-man vehicle had authorized stowage for twenty of the 150mm rockets. (*Christophe Vallier*)

(**Opposite, above**) Based on the much-modified chassis of a Panzer I light tank, industry provided the German army with a flame-thrower version of the vehicle seen here during a demonstration. It was listed as the Sd.Kfz. 122 and nicknamed the 'Flamingo'. The three-man vehicle weighed approximately 27,000lb. The vehicle length was 16ft 1in with a width of 7ft 9in and a height of 6ft 1in. (*Patton Museum*)

(**Opposite, below**) Belonging to the German military museum system is this restored flame-thrower-equipped version of the Panzer III medium tank. Based on the Ausf. M, the 50mm main gun was replaced by a turret-mounted flame gun. The vehicle was fitted with a dummy barrel over the flame projector so as not to betray its purpose on the battlefield, as seen with the vehicle pictured here. (*Andreas Kirchhoff*)

US army soldiers are shown looking over a captured *Flammpanzer* 38(t) *Hetzer* fitted with a dummy main gun barrel. It had on board stowage tanks containing 154 gallons of fuel. Maximum range depending on wind conditions was up to 66 yards. Besides the flame gun, the four-man vehicle was armed with a single machine gun. (*Patton Museum*)

Belonging to a British museum is this preserved Italian flame-thrower vehicle. It was based on the slightly-modified version of the CV-35 tankette, which was typically armed only with machine guns. The two-man vehicle weighed approximately 7,000lb. It was 10ft 1in in length with a width of 4ft 6in and a height of 5ft. (*Tank Museum*)

The *Sturminfanteriegeschütz* (Assault Infantry Gun) 33B pictured here was based on the chassis of the Panzer III medium tank. It was armed with a 150mm howitzer to be employed in close-range urban environments in the direct-fire mode only. The armour on the front of the superstructure was 80mm thick and that on the sides 50mm. (*Patton Museum*)

Coming off the assembly lines after the *Sturminfanteriegeschütz* (Assault Infantry Gun) 33B was the *Sturmpanzer* IV armed with a direct-fire 150mm howitzer. The five-man vehicle was listed as the Sd.Kfz. 166 and had frontal super-structure armour 100mm thick. The sides were 50mm thick. As the restored example pictured here lacks a front glacis-mounted machine gun, it is an early-production unit. (*Paul and Loren Hannah*)

(**Opposite, above**) The most impressive vehicle built for dealing with enemy defensive positions in urban environments was the *Sturmmörser* (Assault Mortar) Tiger pictured here. It was armed with a 380mm mortar that fired two types of rocket-assisted rounds. Frontal armour on the vehicle's superstructure was 150mm thick and that on the sides and rear 80mm. (*Patton Museum*)

(**Opposite, below**) A locally-improvised version of the Panzer I light tank was referred to as the Explosives-Carrier Layer Panzer I Ausf. B. Ten modified units of the tank were fitted with a rear-hull metal framework to which a large explosive charge could be fitted. That explosive charge could then be deposited next to an enemy-built obstacle and exploded to clear the way for assault troops. (*Patton Museum*)

(**Above**) With the fall of France in 1940, the German army acquired thousands of units of the unarmed but armoured French army Renault UE prime movers. The German army armed many of them with machine guns and employed them in France as internal security vehicles such as the example pictured here. Some were later modified to fire rockets, with others armed with small anti-tank guns. (*Ian Wilcox*)

Another pre-war French army unarmoured half-track prime mover employed by the German army was the *Somua MCG*. Most were used as prime movers as the French army had intended. However, as time went on the German army had a number armoured as seen here and armed with a variety of weapons. Their German designation was *Mittlerer Schützenpanzerwagen* (Medium Armoured Infantry Vehicle) S307(f). (*Patton Museum*)

Among the armoured vehicles acquired by the German army upon the fall of France in 1940 was a number of British army Universal Carriers. They were modified to carry a variety of weapons ranging from machine guns to small anti-tank guns. The example pictured in an American museum has been painted to depict how it might have looked in German service. (*Christophe Vallier*)